CRICUT

2 books in 1

The Ultimate Step-by-Step Guide to Start and Mastering Cricut - Cricut for Beginners and Cricut Design Space

Racheal baker

TABLE OF CONTENTS

CRICUT FOR BEGINNER

The Ultimate Step-by-Step Guide To Start and Mastering Cricut, Tools and Accessories and Learn Tips and Tricks to Create Your Perfect Project Ideas

Racheal baker

publisher.

The information herein is offered for informational purposes solely, and is universal as so. The presentation of the information is without contract or any type of guarantee assurance.

The trademarks that are used are without any consent, and the eBook of the trademark is without permission or backing by the trademark owner. All trademarks and brands within this book are for clarifying purposes only and are the owned by the owners themselves, not affiliated with this document.

DISCLAIMER

All erudition contained in this book is given for informational and educational purposes only. The author is not in any way accountable for any results or outcomes that emanate from using this material. Constructive attempts have been made to provide information that is both accurate and effective, but the author is not bound for the accuracy or use/misuse of this information.

FOREWORD

First, I will like to thank you for taking the first step of trusting me and deciding to purchase/read this life-transforming eBook. Thanks for spending your time and resources on this material.

I can assure you of exact results if you will diligently follow the exact blueprint, I lay bare in the information manual you are currently reading. It has transformed lives, and I strongly believe it will equally transform your own life too.

All the information I presented in this Do It Yourself piece is easy to digest and practice.

INTRODUCTION

Want a few cricut thoughts to the cricut cutting device? Cricut private electrical cutters are joining hand crafts and individuals throughout the nation are astonished at the amount of advanced and lovely items they can suddenly create.

The manner a cricut functions is straightforward: simply load a few of many available cartridges to the cutter, choose what colour card stock you'd love to utilize for this specific layout and cut off. Each cartridge has lots of themed layouts - whatever from seasonal layouts to preferred superheroes - and - cricut users may select one or more layouts from every cartridge. The cut out layouts are stuck on...

- Wall hangings
- Scrapbooks
- Image frames
- Custom greeting cards you name it as what is potential using a cricut.

Maybe the absolute most endearing cricut craft thought is a calendar. Another webpage could be made for every month, and every one of those separate pages can be embellished with various layouts. July, for example, will be trimmed using the designs in this independence day seasonal cartridge while february is the most clear option for the love struck seasonal cartridge. The fun does not stop there, however, along with also the mother's day cartridge will be ideal for may while the Easter cartridge is a standard for April. December is unique is cricut-land, also cricut consumers have a lot of collections of layouts such as the joys of the season cartridge along with also the snow friends cartridge to select from.

What would be without scrapbooks to document each and every waking minute of the most prized possessions: our kids? Together with the cricut cutting system, scrapbooks may be customized to each child, and what might be better compared to mom and kid - or dad and kid - to repay together and select which pictures they'd love to decorate their own images with. Cricut also understands that girls and boys are different and this, although the boys probably will not like utilizing the once upon a princess cartridge, they'd go crazy on the batman: the brave and the bold cartridge. Small women, on the other hand, would likely turn their yummy wake up in the robotz cartridge but might love the Disney tinker bell and friends cartridge. You won't ever be at a loss for cricut scrapbooking ideas.

Your cricut design ideas are not only confined to pictures, however, and alphabets will also be available - such as the sesame street font cartridge along with also the ashlyn's alphabet cartridge - them will come in handy when it is time to customize a present. Ideal gifts would comprise images of pets - or possibly vinyl wall-hangings commemorating a special event like this trip abroad - all, needless to say, adorned with bright and beautiful cricut cutouts. Cricut caters to each eventuality, also, here, the produce a critter cartridge along with also the summer at Paris seasonal cartridge will be perfect to match you cricut home decoration.

Birthdays, graduations, Christmas, Hanukkah, bar mitzvahs, baby showers: that the present list is unlimited and this does not even contain those jobs which are completed"just for fun". Cricut has capsules to suit each and every event - and each and every project - which may be considered. Completing a cricut project collectively is also a superb way to get a family to bond, along with the gorgeous things which are created collectively can be cherished for a life.

The Cricut Expression Cutting Machine

The provo craft cricut expression cutting machine is really a huge hit among crafters. It's received a lot of awards and antiques testimonials from several sources. If you're a scrapbooker, teacher, activities director, or anybody else that wants to make paper craft jobs, you are going to want to learn more about the advantages and disadvantages of this cricut expression.

The cricut expression will reduce paper, cardstockvinyl, as well as vellum to shapes, letters, phrases as well as other layouts efficiently. Now you have the choice of employing a 12"x12" cutting mat to get more compact layouts or even the 12"x24" cutting mat to get bigger ones. On the other end of this spectrum, it is possible to cut bits as little as .25", which permits you to consume all these little pieces of paper you have been saving. A variety of lightweight cartridges full of million of designs can be found to expand the Expression's flexibility.

#Cricut Expression vs the Original Cricut

You may have heard concerning the expression's creator, the cricut, also called the'little insect'. The cricut expression utilizes the very same cartridges and knife blades since the first cricut, but permits more versatility. Due to its compact dimensions, the initial cricut is just effective at cutting edge layouts about half of the size of those ones you're able to produce using all the expression. The multiplier additionally has a lot of features not on the first cricut, for example, capability to modify languages and components of dimensions, cut in landscape or portrait view, utilize numerous cuts for thicker fabrics, or produce mirror images employing the other feature. The LCD display is another new feature which lets you see precisely what you'll be cutting until you cut.

The cricut expression has a few disadvantages within the first cricut. The expression is bigger and requires more room on your table or desk. Should you prefer to go to plants or friends' houses to focus on jobs, the plateau is thicker and more awkward to transfer. The expression can be more costly. On the flip side, it enables considerably more flexibility in your layouts. The capacity to reduce larger items is excellent for producing banners or signage and is very helpful to people who must decorate bulletin boards or other large distances.

#Cricut Expression. . .Cutting Edge Technology

In general, that the cricut expression cutting machine is an exciting new solution for crafters. It's particularly nice for those that have arthritis in their hands or whose hands are a bit shaky. Many crafters may find it will not take long to constitute the first price tag of their expression in the sum of money and time that they save from not needing to purchase or cut their layouts. The cost has dropped substantially in the hefty initial retail cost of $499. If you shop carefully, now you can discover the expression for below $300. There's not any computer or high tech understanding required to apply this tricky machine. You can plug it right into any wall socket and plan to begin your job. You'll need to substitute the knife or cutting mat and you might choose to buy extra cartridges to expand your design abilities. It is not a terrible idea to buy the optional instrument kit, possibly, to make the paper a lot easier to lift out of the leading mat. Aside from that, the expression is nearly carefree. As soon as you have a cricut expression cutting machine, then it will become such an essential part of your crafting, so you may wonder how you ever got along without it.

Greatest strategies for selecting the ideal cricut personal electronic cutter

The array of cricut personal electronic cutter machines was made to automate a number of the fiddly crafting jobs. If you have never heard of these before, then keep reading to learn how to choose your house crafts into another level. In case you know of these, you might be asking yourself how to choose which of those cutting machines will be suitable for you. Within the following guide, i'll be assisting you to choose which of those four cricut versions is the very best match for your needs. In the procedure, you are going to observe the advantages and disadvantages of every machine, to assist you in making an educated choice.

The four versions we are going to be studying would be the normal cricut personal electronic cutter, the cricut produce, " the cricut expression along with also the cricut cake.

The simplest model to check at first is your cricut cake. This differs to others, as it's made with one goal in mind. That's, to make professional looking decorations . It may cut shapes out of bread, fondant, gum paste along with other raw materials. It's extremely much like this cricut expression system, but the working components are changed to make them appropriate for food. That means components which have to be washed can be readily eliminated. If you're searching to make edible decorations, then this is the only choice in the scope. This version retails from approximately $270.

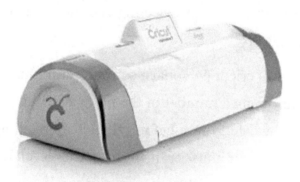

The additional three cricut personal electronic cutter versions are suitable for home printing. They cut from the very same materials, including paper, vinyl, card and vellum. Which version you choose is going to depend upon your budget and requirements.

#budget

The normal cricut personal electronic cutter is the lowest

priced in the scope, costing a minimum of about $100.

Next up is your cricut generate, coming in at $160 and upward.

The surface of the range version is that the cricut expression, that will put you back around $225.

Prerequisites

All versions are compatible with the entire selection of cricut cartridges. This usually means you have an almost infinite supply of cutting edge layouts, since you could always buy more capsules. Therefore there are two important facets in your needs to push your choice. These will be the dimensions of cuts and machine, as well as the assortment of cutting edge choices.

- The conventional personal electronics cutter and make machines are small and mobile. They'll cut contours around approximately 11.5 inches. The produce has a considerably wider assortment of cutting edge purposes.

- The expression is a bigger machine, made to get a permanent spot in a desk or workbench. It'll cut contours around approximately 23.5 inches, and with a large assortment of cutting edge functions.

- By considering these concerns, you ought to have the ability to choose that cricut personal electronic cutter is just the only one for you.

Cricut projects - ideas that may generate income

People really feel the cricut machine is the 1 instrument that's responsible for the conceptualization of these layouts which people see in scrapbooks. In fact, the designs are derived in the brain of the consumer and are made concrete by the cricut cutting device.

In addition, additionally, there are other tools which help make the layouts such as capsules and software applications. The top software tool out there's that the cricut design studio. With this application, you can create and edit your own layouts and also edit current designs which are pre - packed.

Life is great really! People also believe the use of an cricut cutting system is simply restricted to the area of scrapbooking. Not a lot of men and women know of the but there that the cricut machine in addition to the cartridges along with the software tools may be used to get a large number of items. There are a whole lot of cricut projects which you are able to use the cricut cutting system for and just your brain can restrict what you could do.

Greeting cards are excellent cricut projects for anybody to participate in. Together with the layouts which you are able to receive from the cricut cartridge along with the software tools which you have set up, you layout covers which withstand the unconventional. The difficulty that most men and women experience when they attempt to buy greeting cards is that nearly all of the point is they can't locate the plan of this card which they are interested in finding. This may induce anxiety and a great deal of frustration about the purchaser's part. You're a lot better off making your personal greeting cards.

Cricut calendars are another fantastic idea to get a cricut cutting device. A calendar is full of 12 weeks. It is possible to get creative and search for layouts on your cartridge or software which could reflect the entire month that's inside your calendar. If we're at the month of december, then you may search for layouts that fit the mood and feeling of december. Start looking for snowmen, reindeers, and christmas trees. I promise you that you have all of the layouts you will ever desire within your own software or catridge.

Bear in mind, just your imagination can restrict what you do. These cricut projects may be utilized either for private fulfillment or revenue generating functions. Be imaginative with your chosen machine. You never understand what crazy and crazy thoughts can pop in to your mind.

Complex cricut suggestions for the craft project

Cricut private cutters are carrying hand crafts to another new degree. People throughout the nation are astonished at the amazing and advanced cricut thoughts this machine may bring to a project listing. You may create virtually anything amazing and one of a type employing the cricut cartridges.

How does one cricut machine function? It is very straightforward. Simply put in a cricut cartridge to the machine, then choose what colour card stock that you would like to utilize for your individual layout and cut off. Each chance has different themed layouts from seasonal layouts to popular cartoon characters. You are able to pick in the cut designs out to use for decorations, picture frames, picture frames, customized greeting cards, wall hangings, calendars and a lot more.

One of the amazing cricut thoughts you are able to create as the craft is your cricut calendar. Every month can be produced in another page and you may decorate these pages using various layouts. Could not it be wonderful to make your february webpage working with the love struck season cartridge? The easter cartridge will supply you with unlimited layouts to the april page calendar. Your may calendar could be made in the mother's day cartridge. How interesting is it to style your july webpage with trimmings made in the independence day season cartridge? December could be equipped together with all the joys of the season cartridge along with snow friends cartridge. You are able to select for your heart's content.

Another fantastic idea you'll be able to possibly make is your scrapbook. This well-loved craft project is why cricut cutting machine has been devised in the first location. Together with the cricut cutting system, you can customize decorations to your kids, such as mother-daughter or dad and child keepsake. Cricut created capsules which each tiny child would delight in making like the once upon a princess cartridge or even the Disney tinker bell and friends cartridge. Your small super hero will certainly love the batman layout in the batman: the brave and the bold or robotz cartridges. Cricut provides you humungous layouts to select from to the scrapbooking ideas.

The cricut layouts aren't merely lay out thoughts but additionally fonts and alphabets in the sesame street font cartridge along with also the Ashlyn's alphabet cartridge. Use these exciting tools after making your personalized gift like a wall-hanging image frame of having a photograph of a memorable occasion of the receiver of your gift. Embellish your walls hanging with quite cutouts produced by the cricut cutter.

Your cricut thoughts are endless by means of the great machine and also the cricut capsules to match any event and project which it is possible to consider. Creating a cricut project with the entire family is a superb way to spend some time together and producing those gorgeous items can be a terrific experience for everyone to achieve.

Cricut manual for beginners and advanced users

How to utilize the cricut? Basically you add the cartridge,

then set the rubber crucial overlay on the keyboardand turn the device on, then stick a piece of 6 inch paper into the mat which accompanies the device (be certain that you line this up using the tiny arrow onto the mat) press on the"load paper" button and then feed the mat/paper to the machine, then press on the key(s) you to get what you would like to reduce and press on the"cut" button.

If you are a complete novice, you ought to get a scrapbook record with protective sheets (they're fairly affordable, you do not really have to receive the pricey ones). A good colour is generally best, such as black, royal blue . In addition they have patterned/designed ones.

* You should find any paper (12x12, 8x8, 6x6 etc..) not too pricey ($2-4 packs)

* you should find some adhesives to adhere photographs to newspaper (do not use adhesive sticks, so they tend to lift paper and jumble it up) ($.99-3.99)

* get your hands on vases (for example, ribbon, stickers, brads etc) (ranges from $.99-4.99)

* find pencils, archival safe, (such as journaling, be certain they don't bleed, blot) ($2.99-8.99+) sakura jelly rolls, zig millennium, zig memory system, marvy etc..) are fantastic brands & won't ruin paper .

* get your pick dimensions of scrapbook album (6x6, 8x8, 12x12) not pricey ($5.99-19.99) a fantastic dimension to start off would be an 8x8. Approx $7 to this

* receive a newspaper trimmer: to cut extra borders in photographs or reduce paper into a particular dimension ($8.99-19.99)

All these are only the basic items. Do not let shoppers urge choose the very best of you. It happens to most people scrapbookers. We see something adorable that we enjoy but not use it don't want it. Check for earnings. Use coupons in the event that you're able to. Check shops such as the.99 penny stores that also sell rolling sheets for a inexpensive cost & its exactly the exact same thing because the glue you'd locate in michaels for $4-7. Walmart also includes a part of scrapbooking things cheaper than local craft shops (michaels, joanns, hobby lobby etc)

Assess ebay too. There is lots of inexpensive priced things to get.

How To/What to perform precisely:

1. Choose the paper that you would like to utilize. 2. The photograph that you need to add to newspaper. (be certain the

surplus sections of photograph are cut off--to get a nicer appearance utilize your paper trimmer. 3. Utilizing your rolling glue (or"dots") operate it via corners of picture (do not need much only corners & centre). 4. Place picture in newspaper where you wish to. 5. Put any embellishment you might need to decorate it. (this component enables you to be as imaginative as you would like to be.) 6. Journal whatever nice/fun to keep in mind from anything occur or proceeded in that picture. 7. In case you have anything such as brochures, ticket stub or anything, then set them. Make webpages look nicer also.

With countless possibilities using cricut software

The official cricut applications, also called cricut design studio, is a form of software especially designed to create cutting pictures simpler. Using an easy thumb drive apparatus (USB), then you'll have the instantaneous benefit of producing all the layouts which you need that may be cut employing a cricut device. This is just the fastest and handiest link which you may ever need for the your pc and cricut.

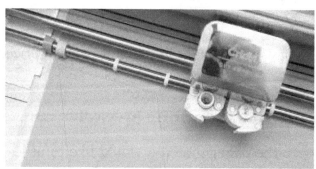

With the support of this Cricut program, you'll have the

ability to produce many designs for any project which you are thinking about. You'll have the advantage of welding, resizing, reshaping, blending as well as twisting pictures of your selection. These attributes alone can provide you more independence and flexibility which you have ever believed possible. On top of that, you don't have to be a genius or a specialist to have the ability to accomplish and make your crafts crafts.

Cricut design studio supposed to provide all craftspeople innumerable advantages. Among those advantages is how the app was pre-loaded with each and every cartridge available for your cricut cutters. This means about a million of distinct designs and patterns which you could use since it's or combine with each other to make a more lovely, distinctive and lavish cutting layouts. Consider the infinite possibilities it's possible to invent, the million of layouts you'll be able to develop. It is possible to also do mixes with your pals.

Now, you might have qualms about getting your self this program since you may consider the approaching new patterns which are going to be available later on. Disregard this notion! Among the most important and funniest advantages of cricut applications is that after you've bought via their official site, you simply must check for newest updates once every so often. When there's a brand new upgraded routine, you do not need to purchase another program to have a hold of this, you just only update your present software and you are all set. The thing which you need to recall here is that irrespective of the amount of designs which you produce, these will just be trimmed and created with the capsules which you have available. However, you don't need to be worried because the cricut will ask you to fit the compulsory cartridge which you need to utilize for your self-improvement routines.

Just imagine the number of jobs which you're able to be in a position to perform with cricut applications. As stated previously, you do not have to be an authority in digital imaging to use this program. This is very fantastic news for novices who hesitate to utilize unique kinds of crafting applications. The very best thing about this particular toll is that it has an interface that's totally user friendly. You are able to easily get the hang of it before you know it, you'll be hooked on utilize the applications with each combination you can consider. There are almost no limitations to what you may design and produce with this program. So go ahead, try cricut and then begin your own scrapbooking adventure.

CHAPTER ONE
WHAT IS CRICUT?

C ricut is your brand-name of a merchandise array of home die-cutting machines (or cutting plotters) utilized for scrapbooking and assorted endeavors, created from Provo Craft & Novelty, Inc. (also known as"Provo Craft") of Spanish Fork, Utah. The machines have been used for cutting paper, felt, vinyl, cloth and other items like fondant. Cricut is one of many digital die cutters utilized by newspaper crafters, card makers and scrapbookers.

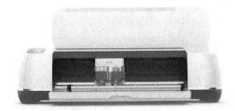

Models

The initial cricut machine needed cutting coasters of 6 × 12 inches, the much bigger cricut explorer simply lets mats of 12 × 12 and 12 × 24. The biggest machine will create letters by a half inch to 23½ inches . The cricut along with cricut explorer air two demand mats and blades that may be corrected to cut various varieties of paper, vinyl and other sheet solutions. The cricut private paper cutter functions as a paper filler predicated upon cutting edge parameters programmed into the system, and looks like a printer. Cricut cake creates stylized edible fondants cut various shapes in fondant sheets, also can be used by chefs at the groundwork and ornamentation of all cakes.

Present Models

These versions are now compatible with the present cricut design space program.

Cricut research 1

The explore it's really a wired die cutting tool which can cut an assortment of materials from paper to cloth and much more. Be aware: there's a wireless bluetooth adapter available for sale individually. This machine just had one instrument slot machine compared with other currently supported versions which have 2.

Cricut research air

The explore air is really a wireless die cutting machine that may cut many different materials from paper to cloth and much more. This system is basically the same as its next iteration, aside from the home and slower cutting skills.

Cricut research air two

The explore air two is small refresh of this research air line that included three colours (mint blue, rose anna, giffin lilac) in addition to a quick mode to reduce back vinyl, iron-on, and card inventory at"around 2x speeds"

Cricut maker

The cricut maker is really a brand new lineup on august 20, 2017, made to cut heavier materials like balsa wood, basswood, non-bonded cloth, leather, and sensed.

The maker is your sole cricut machine which supports the usage of a blade for cutting edge cloth directly, and also a steering wheel with varying pressure to score heavier papers compared to the initial scoring stylus.

Legacy machines

First cricut

The first cricut has a 6" x 12" cutting mat and graphics can be trimmed in a range between 1" into 5 1/2" tall. The first cricut can be used with original cricut cartridges. The first cricut doesn't have the capability to cut many distinct kinds of materials the newer cricut machines may. But, cricut does create a deep cut blade & housing that may allow initial cricut owners to reduce stuff around 1.55mm thick, for example bark, chipboard, and postage materials. The first cricut can also be compatible with all the cricut design craft room.

Cricut expression

The cricut expression® provides several benefits over the former version. To begin with, it permits users to reduce shapes and fonts in a variety between 1/4" into 231/2", and has a 12" x 12" cutting edge with flexible slides so users no longer will need to trim down their media to 6" x 12". It cuts a larger assortment of substances, such as vellum, cloth, chipboard, vinyl, and thin foils. Additionally, it offers an lcd display to preview the job, and contains features such amount and auto-fill. Even a"paper saver" style and selection of portrait or landscape orientation also have been included. The fundamental version has two capsules within the buy, plantin schoolbook along with accent essentials.

Cricut picture

This system was completely unique because it had an hp 97 ink jet printer built to it that it may either cut and publish pictures. This system had a revamped touch screen interface, also has been extremely big and heavy. The device had a very short lifetime of nearly 1 year.

Cricut expression two

The cricut length 2 includes an upgraded exterior from that the cricut expression. It includes a 12" x 12" cutting mat. This system doesn't have the keyboard the first cricut along with also the cricut expression consumed. Rather it sports a brand new full-color lcd touch display. The lcd touch screen shows the computer keyboard on the display and lets you view where your pictures are going to be on the mat before cutting. Additionally, it has the newest characteristic of independent picture sizing and picture turning directly over the lcd display.

Cricut mini

The cricut mini is a tiny private electronic cutting machine. Unlike another cricut machines it simply works using a pc, it cannot cut pictures standing independently. You need to utilize cricut craft room layout computer software. The cricut mini includes over 500 pictures which are automatically unlocked once you join your cricut using all the cricut craft room design applications or your cricut gypsy apparatus. The machine will not have a cartridge jack that's compatible with cricut cartridges except that the cricut picture capsules. The cricut mini also offers a exceptional mat dimensions of 8.5" x 12". The cricut mini may cut pictures in a selection of 1/4" into 11 1/2". Even the cricut mini relied solely on utilizing cricut craft room, a computer software which no longer works. Of the legacy cricut machines, the mini is the only person which is outdated and not usable at all. As no recourse has been supplied to the clients who had bought cartridges for that system, provo-craft has become the focus of several complaints for clients who had been left without a recourse with this sudden pressured'sun-setting' of this machine.

Cartridges

Designs are produced from components saved on capsules . Each cartridge includes a computer keyboard overlay and education booklet. The plastic computer keyboard overlay suggests key collections for this chance only. Nevertheless lately provo craft has published a"universal overlay" which can be used with cartridges released after august 1, 2013. The objective of the universal overlay would be to simplify the practice of clipping by simply needing to learn 1 keyboard overlay rather than being required to find out the overlay for every individual cartridge. Designs could be cut on a pc using all the cricut design studio applications, on a USB attached gypsy device, or could be directly inputted onto the cricut device employing the computer keyboard overlay. There are two forms of cartridges font and shape. Each cartridge has many different creative attributes which could allow for countless distinct cuts from only 1 cartridge. There are over 275 capsules which can be found (separately from the system), including shapes and fonts, together with new ones added each month. When some cartridges are standard in articles, cricut includes licensing arrangements including Disney, pixar, nickelodeon, sesame street, dc comics along with hello kitty. The cricut lineup includes a variety of costs, but the capsules are synonymous, but not all choices on a cartridge might be accessible with the more compact machines. All cartridges work just with cricut applications, needs to be registered to one user to be used and can't be offered or given away. A cartridge bought for a stop machine is very likely to turn into useless in the point that the machine is stopped. Cricut reserves the right to stop support for a number of versions of the applications at any moment, which may make some capsules instantly obsolete.

What Can Be A Cricut Machine?

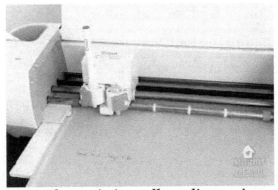

The Cricut Explore Air is really a die-cutting system (aka craft plotter or cutting edge system). You can Consider it such as a printer; you also make an image or layout in your own personal computer and Then ship it to your device. Except that Rather than printing your layout, the Cricut machine cuts out of whatever substance you desire! The cricut research air can reduce paper, vinyl, cloth, craft foam, decal paper, faux leather, and longer !

In reality, if you would like to utilize a cricut just like a printer, then it may do this also! There's an attachment slot on your system and you're able to load a mark in there after which possess the cricut"draw" the layout for you. It is ideal for obtaining a stunning handwritten look if your design is not all that good.

The cricut explore air may reduce stuff around 12″ broad and includes a little cutting blade mounted within the system. When you are prepared to cut out something, you load the stuff on a sticky mat and then load the mat to your machine. The mat holds the material in place while the cricut blade moves over the substance and cuts . If it finishes, then you unload the mat in the machine, then peel off your project the mat, and then you are all set to move!

Using a cricut system, the options are infinite! All you want is a cricut system, design space, some thing to reduce, along with your creativity!

What could I do with a cricut machine?

There are a lot of things you can perform using a cricut device! There is no way that I could list all of the possibilities, however, here are a couple popular kinds of jobs to provide you a good concept about exactly what the machine could perform.

· cut out interesting shapes and letters to get cartoon

· make habit, handmade cards for any specific event (here is an illustration)

· layout a onesie or some t-shirt (here is an illustration)

· create a leather necklace

· create buntings and other party decorations

· make your own stencils for painting (here is an illustration)

· create a plastic decal for your vehicle window

· tag material on your cabinet, or in a playroom

· make monogram cushions

· make your own christmas decorations (here is an illustration)

· address an envelope

· decorate a mugcup, or tumbler (here is an illustration)

· etch glass at house (here is an illustration)

· make your own wall stickers

· create a painted wooden signal

· create your own window

· cut appliqués or quilt squares

· produce stickers to get a rack mixer

...and plenty of different jobs which are too many to list!

Do It Yourself Using A Cricut Cutter

The cricut cutter is not for everybody. It's not right for the man or woman who's just a casual crafter. It doesn't make any difference if you're a beginner or an advanced crafter it's for the man or woman who's seriously interested in paper crafting. It's a sizable

investment if you don't want to keep busy in document crafting. You sometimes can come across a cutter produce for about $100 in the event that you appear online. This cost can occasionally create the cricut cutter overly pricey for all. As you think about all of the decals, pre-packaged bling, pre-cut letters, numbers, and shapes many scrapbook fans discover the more dedicated scrappers find it eventually cover itself. It's possible to make personalized invitations, gift tags and christmas cards, and then pack and sell them to recover the cost of this cricut. It's by provo craft plus they have a good standing in workmanship, and their products are frequently known to be quite durable, together with replacement components available if desired.

with your own cricut cutter it is a lot less difficult to cut through just about any type or feel of paper. You may also create your own paper, so allow it to dry completely, and then media with your iron (no steam). You are able to use your paper to make real one of a kind cards or scrapbooks and among your kind antiques. Things nobody else has or may understand how to replicate regardless of how hard they try. This will permit your layouts to make original scrapbooks employing a number of shades and textures which may not be replicated.

Experiment together with your cricut cutter. Create new

form and color combinations to permit something distinctive and unforgettable to be found. Shhhhhh... Here's a key tip: following your letter or number or form was trimmed together with your cricut cutter, gently hold the newspaper and choose a tiny rigid craft paint brush, then dip in to future floor wax, also paint the newspaper in which you want the feel to be odd. Let it dry to a plastic plate. Now you can do this a couple times or until you're pleased with the outcome. The newspaper changes feel. Cricut cutter machines have been exceptionally flexible, simple to use, and imaginative enough to be utilized for almost any paper craft project.

A cricut cutter can produce pictures which are "to more than 5" tall. Easy to change capsules are utilized to include customized characters, intriguing boundaries, festive shapes, trendy phrases all made by you to represent your private content of a webpage. Chipboard shouldn't be used or you may hurt the blades. You ought to keep tabs on the sharpness of the blade so that you may have a replacement if necessary. Heavier caliber of cardstock may also result in blades to dull faster. This usually means you'll have the chance to purchase the less expensive paper or cardstock.

- Cricut cartridges sale - the way to save huge on cricut cartridges
- A cricut cartridges purchase is similar to a birthday and christmas morning to most cricut users

including novices, beginners or innovative masters.

What Is The Very Best Form Of Cartridge Purchase?

One sale that must not be overlooked is one which features variety. The chance sale which simply can not be passed is one which supplies a huge array of cartridges, like themes and fonts.

For example, by purchasing a couple versatile cartridges such as the beyond birthdays cartridge, alphalicous cartridge and also among those pick disney cartridges, developing a customized card or scrapbook is an absolute breeze. These cartridges offer you extreme flexibility, together with an amazing font, images for special events and some of those much-loved disney personalities to boot up.

The point is a cricut cartridges sale may be the ideal chance to expand a set and in doing this, expand a design that is creative.

Revenue are an ideal time to find the most bang from this dollar. Cartridges, as precious as they are, can certainly accumulate. By taking complete benefit of a circuit breaker purchase, these brand new cartridges are going to be well worth every cent, particularly after making countless names, tags and scrapbook pages.

Cricut wedding undertaking

Here are some fantastic cricut project ideas for creating fantastic homemade greeting cards. This project is for a marriage. It's ideal for giving to a person as a congratulations card to their wedding parties.

Beneath is a listing of items you'll need.

O cardstock: snowy

O patterned paper: purple, pink

O buttons: purple love hearts

O photos of the bride and groom

O pink ribbon

O glue

Directions:

1. Cut a wonderful thick square box. Utilizing graphically speaking orange and cartridge patterned paper, then press shift and reduce on one 4".

2. Cut the name block. Employing the pink cardstock, cut on one 4". Repeat cut employing the purple newspaper.

3. Cut laptop background. Employing the pink patterned paper, then press shift and reduce on one 4".

4. Stick the photos of the groom and bride on the card.

5. Adhere to pink love hearts round the picture of the bridge

and groom.

6. Connect the pink ribbon into a bow then attach the bow on the card.

7. Insert the text such as:"congratulations sarah and richard in your wedding from jean and paul along with loved ones! Xxx"

This need to choose between half an hour and twenty five moments depending how experienced you're using a cricut device. This cricut project thought is really depending on the creative understanding of novices so this isn't a professional cricut job.

Please notice you'll also want:

Recall you may always try various notions you do not have to follow along with the project tutorial step in which you could always alter the color scheme a bit and change the dimensions of this card .

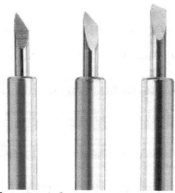

Great Luck with your job!

The base camp cricut chance is a ribbon cartridge that's fantastic for scrapbooks, stationary and people all-important commemorations honoring our servicemen and servicewomen. With decoration and assorted designs that match a broad selection of jobs, cricut novices and experts should take a peek at what the base camp cricut cartridge has to offer you.

7 Base Camp Cricut Cartridge Tips

1. The base camp chance is about endurance, endurance and flexibility. With these qualities in your mind, users may benefit as much or as little as they need from this innovative instrument. The crucial thing is to make the most of this cartridge offers, so understanding it from top to base.

2. The ribbon is a simple alphabet, with this extraneous glitz within different fonts. It consistently contains numerals 0-9 and many symbols that are common. Using a straightforward and traditional font like this one, consumers may use it in almost any capacity. Use it to get the two formal jobs and ones which are only for pleasure.

3. Together with the ribbon, in addition, there are a number of graphic phrases. These include: " I miss you, kiss kiss hug hug, i(heart)u4evr, thank you, happy birthday, usa, as well as the, to and from. These heartfelt sentiments may be used to

get a huge array of motives, but since the title would imply, each one these graphical phrases may be utilized to enjoying thoughts and prayers to our troops.

4. Another tip would be to utilize the cartridge to make personalized cards, invitations, and thank you notes as well as present tags for nearest and dearest. By employing the images, in addition to the innovative attributes, making such things is a breeze.

5. Another suggestion is to utilize all that's featured within this innovative tool to make handmade picture frames for the closest friends and nearest and dearest. Pick out a couple of your favourite cartridge phrases such as"kiss kiss hug hug" and"i(heart)u4evr" and then set them along the borders of the framework.

6. The base camp cartridge includes several creative alternatives that may be used to include shapes and much more to a paper crafts. These attributes include: label, dog tag,

appeal, shadow, rectangle and much more.

7. With these innovative attributes, users can quickly create their dog tags and allure. To get gift-wrapping and celebrations, users may also use those attributes to create place cards, name tags and prefer tags.

With so much to provide, it's no surprise that individuals everywhere are visiting that the cricut base camp cartridge to the flexible and functional tool it is. Produce something private with all the base camp cricut chance and also these 7 helpful hints.

Cricut cartridge - remembrance of holidays past

This season with the assistance of all cricut cartridge, start a brand new holiday tradition by collecting your zest to get a nostalgic family record. Provo craft cricut capsules give a hand in assisting you to create designer fashion scrapbook pages.

The scrapbook craze swept america in the civil war into the 1880s fueled from the vibrant pictures and folds up scenes of vacation collectibles that recipients desired to maintain and exhibit. The scrapbooks functioned as cherished reminders as the decades pass.

Beautiful illustrated postcards in the 19th century have been thrown off in temples for safekeeping. Historians follow holiday greeting cards into 18th century schoolboys who wrote intricate letters for their parents to demonstrate their improvement created in penmanship.

In the olden times, scrapbookers painstakingly pasted the attractively decorated calendars and cards into records using an alternative made from bread and water. Antique cards are still appeal now. An collection of early 1900s published postcards exemplifies memories brought to life and maintained in history.

Nowadays, using cricut cartridge names like calligraphy collection and jasmine capsules, it is possible to provide that old world design feel to your present art endeavors. Contain sourcing and paper clippings for an individual touch.

Seven Easy Steps To Completing The Fantastic Scrapbook Page:

- Select a motif.
- Co-ordinate newspapers.
- Crop photographs.
- Mat pictures.
- Page design.
- Create name and diary.

Insert memorabilia and antiques.

* Die cut letters produce a fast name or going for almost any design.

* pictures can be obsolete or garnished with chalks or

emphasized with gel pens.

* a shadow effect may be only created by clipping out the exact same letter in two distinct colours.

* the contours can then be overlapped, permitting the underside color to show through.

* use leftover bits for cutting letters out to lessen waste.

For finishing a particular scrapbook, pick a set of photos or just one big photo to your front cover. On account of this huge cricut cartridge catalog, the novice scrapbooker might be readily overwhelmed.

The great news is that modern scrapbooking is now a communal previous moment. Finding inspiration from other scrappers and hints on that cricut cartridges will probably work great for you is an easy click away.

Opposites bring, storybook, and wild card chance are simply a couple of the wonderful choices available to help you in your trip for remembrance of vacations past.

What exactly does cricut cartridges need to offer you?

There are all sorts of cricut capsules that anybody can utilize. These cartridges work in several types and are designed to take care of an assortment of distinct products. They are also able to be simple to handle at a cricut apparatus. The characteristics that include these capsules are remarkable and must be utilised to make some fine styles that anybody can handle.

All these cricut capsules are all created using the exact same bodily layouts. This is done to make it a lot easier for an individual to load and then remove a cartridge out of a cricut apparatus. The crucial thing is to maintain the magnetic characteristics that connect the chance into the apparatus clean and simple to control. This is indeed that the cartridge will keep working and it could.

A cartridge will contain two important points. To begin with, it is going to feature a unique font. This font may relate to a particular theme and may incorporate both upper and lower case items as well as some numbers and special characters.

The cartridge may also incorporate a collection of shapes and images. These can be different by every cartridge. These ought to be viewed to make nice looks which are cut correctly and equally if the cricut machine functions correctly.

The topics that cricut cartridges may include are extremely appealing. These capsules may include things like topics which vary from traditional holiday motifs to ones which deal with specific interests such as flowers, animals, sports and other items. The assortment of cricut capsules that anybody can locate is so enormous it might take some time to list all of the available choices.

each cartridge may also incorporate a great keyboard design that will examine the computer keyboard onto the cricut apparatus. This is utilized to aid with distributing advice on which the particular kind of layout may be. It's designed to keep things recorded carefully and to make sure that data is made to where it is not going to be too much hassle to handle.

A number of those distinctive cartridges may also incorporate items which work with various colours in your mind. Included in these are layouts in which the appearance can match along with specific paper colours. A complete guide may be utilized to indicate that paper things which have to be used carefully. This ought to be handled to maintain things looking as good as they are sometimes.

There are a number of those capsules that may work with particular designs taken for classroom requirements. By way of instance, 1 alternative can use a layout which permits a consumer to produce cutouts of fifty countries. Designs may also be built to cut cursive letters to ensure it is simpler for pupils to understand to operate with specific procedures of writing in school. The layouts can be exceptional but they ought to be assessed carefully.

People should consider how cricut cartridges may operate in several types. These layouts are created to produce some great looks which are created to maintain all sorts of functions working nicely regardless of what types of things one must manage.

Which Are Cricut Machines And Why Are They So Popular?

Cricut machines have altered the world of crafting. These machines are particularly popular with crafters since they're fun, easy to use, and also conserve punctually. If you like to decorate and craft, all these machines are a must have! There are lots of versions of cricut machines in provo craft including the expression, expression two, picture, private cutter, mini, gypsy, produce, cake, cake mini, along with martha stewart crafts edition. There's a die cutting tool which will suit you and your kind crafting.

All these machines will provide you exact die cuts each moment. No longer cutting edge and crafting by hand. This saves an immense quantity of time, and that means that you are able to begin on additional projects you have not had the opportunity to enter. You may work on multiple jobs at precisely the exact same time should you would like. Cricut machines paired together with the countless themed cricut cartridges accessible from provo craft offer you unlimited chances for your creative side.

Cricut machines supplies a huge array of cartridges for almost any event you can consider. The expense of the cartridges vary from $25 to around $60 per year. These capsules have fonts and graphics which could be customized for all of your endeavors. You might even change the textures and colours of your own materials and achieve unique looks with your endeavors utilizing exactly the identical cartridge. In case you have family or friends which likewise craft using cricut machines it's possible to swap or borrow capsules to save cash.

Cricut machines could be bought online or in a craft shop. Obviously, the cost depends upon the version you decide on. Their cost can vary anywhere from $100 to $350 generally. On some occasions, it is possible to discover excellent deals hunting on the internet for revenue or locate a secondhand one. As soon as you discover the model that's ideal for you, then you ought to create a note regarding what tools are included with that. On occasion you'll have to acquire tools along with this equipment for example cutting off mats, spatula, replacement blades, blades, and needless to cutting stuff for your own project.

As you're able to view these machines really are a substantial investment, but may be quite rewarding and enjoyable for a long time to come. Any crafter may gain in the high-tech inventions and professional-looking jobs regardless of if you're a beginner or pro crafter. Amaze your family and friends with your imagination. Make crafting creative and fun again using cricut machines.

Everything you want to know about the cricut personal cutter before purchasing

Before investing your hard earned cash to a die cutting platform, you have to do your own research. There are numerous versions available on the industry and after much thought this is actually the oneI've selected and why.

The cricut personal cutter system made by Provo craft is a wonderful edition for your own scrapbooking tools. There are some distinct cricut personal cutters. The cricut expressions will reduce 12x 24 inch dimension newspapers. The cricut original cuts 6x12 inch newspaper. Even the cricut cutting mat includes a gentle adhesive and retains your paper in position although the cutting edge is done. Every cricut machine includes a cartridge, so the cricut original includes george & basic shapes and it's a basic cartridge, which unites capital alphabet named george along with a choice of shapes. Each cartridge is made up of capsule, a keypad overlay plus a few include the instruction booklet. So as soon as you've got unpacked your new cricut personal cutter you may begin experimenting immediately away. Down the monitor you further extend the performance of your cricut system, together with other cricut capsules. Provocraft is publishing new cricut cartridges annually and they have broad selection of topics, from alphabets, sports, even in the backyard through to Disney characters.

On that the cricut personal cutter it's possible to correct blade thickness, stress and cutting rate. This assists when cutting different substances. Slowing down the cutting edge rate gives a much better outcome with more delicate scrapbooking paper, even whilst using moderate pressure provides a crisper cut scrapbooking cardstock rather than the softest stress setting.

You can cut shapes and letters by adjusting the dimensions dial from 1 to 5 1/2 inch. The sizes available are 1, 1 11/4, 11/22, two, two 1/2, 3, 31/2, 4, 5 41/2551/2.

The capability to load up the scrapbooking paper, then cut a couple of letters, then unload the newspaper and reload to precisely the point you had been around, saves the time and paper.

The cricut cartridge george along with basic shapes includes six innovative capabilities. Signal up, slotted, charm, silhouette, shadow and shadow blackout.

Signal - envision that a picket sign with a letter or form cut

Slotted - oval ring, a slot clip in the very top to thread ribbon or twine

Charm - your letter or shape cut using a ring attached at the top, so you can join the correspondence using a brad for your design

Silhouette - cuts that the outline of your own letter or form. Great for the budget conscious as you're in a position to maintain the adverse cut of your correspondence and use it on a different design.

Shadow - cuts the letters or contours, slightly bigger than ordinary, these can subsequently be utilized behind the standard dimensions correspondence, giving the look of a shadow along with a 3d effect for your name. This attribute is on each one the cricut capsules.

Cricut sampler cricut cartridge - 7 tips you can use now

The cricut sampler cricut cartridge is easily among the most adored capsules in the full collection and together with"cricut sampler cricut cartridge - 7 tips you can use now," users know seven reasons why this inventive tool never gets older.

The finest way to describe this particular cartridge would be by describing others. The cricut sampler chance is comprised of images and graphics from various well-known cartridges. Initially the chance was created as the greatest starter thing and a trailer of sorts for different capsules. But users immediately realized they got the very best of many worlds and may take advantage of the smorgasbord of images.

Cartridges Contained from the Cricut Sampler cartridge

comprise: Makin' the Grade, Walk into My Backyard, New Arrival, Paper Pups, Opposites Attract, Moving Location, Alphalicious, Fabulous Finds, ZooBalloo, and Printing Press.

Cricut Sampler Cricut Cartridge - 7 Tips You Can Use Now

1. See to the sampler as precisely what it really is! As soon as you've got it, don't adhere to one or 2 of your favourite pictures. Rather, try out just a small bit of what, experimentation and determine why provocraft believed that these capsules were significant enough to turn into a sampler.

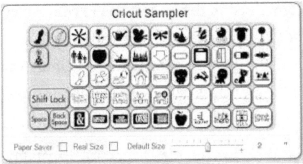

2. Create your own personalized static! This cartridge contains all you want to create a magical and whimsical group of letterheads, envelopes and notes.

3. Produce cards, such as thank you cards, invitations, congratulatory notes, solidarity cards and even cards simply to say hello. With this specific cartridge, it's about just how creative you are using the graphics and images available.

4. Make the most of those phrases. Phrases contain words

such as love, thank you, you are invited, you are the greatest, I miss you, it is a party, joy, limited edition, top secret, number 1 student, number 1,, friends forever, family, love, woof and much more! Add them into pre-made things or produce your own creations.

5. Produce your own gift tags with the assistance of all the particular capabilities. Using the aid of button, then you may make tags and readily distort them together with all the pictures and colors included here.

6. As soon as you've taken advantage of this cricut sampler cricut cartridge, then have a look at another cricut capsules that are showcased in this one. If you're completely satisfied with all the cricut sampler cricut cartridge, then do not bother with others. But in the event that you simply can not get enough of those images, simply have a look at the complete capsules.

7. Make the most of the distinctive capabilities. These attributes may be used to add exceptional effects, such as shadows that add depth to pictures.

The cricut sampler cricut cartridge is exceptional in that, although it's a sampler capsule, it may stand alone on its own as a result of its unbelievable group of pictures. Users may use this cartridge offers and what it does not. Currently, with the assistance of all cricut sampler cricut cartridge.

Cricut Suggestions - Tips About How Best to Make the Most

of Your Own Cricut Machine

The cricut machine was produced for a large number of factors. Now most folks might feel this gadget is exclusively for producing scrapbooks . However, it isn't. The cricut machine may be used for entire lot more of stuff than simply making scrapbooks. If you seem closes in a cricut machine and you also allow your creativity go crazy, you can think of a great deal of great cricut thoughts which could enable you to own a supply of simple or living give your private satisfaction.

As what has been mentioned before, folks associate the usage of a cricut system using only making scrapbooks. Among those excellent cricut ideas which are worth discussing is a cricut machine may also be utilised to make calendars that are fantastic. The cricut machine in addition to the cricut design studio program may be utilized to produce layouts for your own calendar.

One calendar year is constituted of 12 weeks. Please note that every month consistently has a theme for this as being moist, chilly, and there may even be weeks which are noteworthy for a particular occasion. Together with the 2 tools which we just said, it is possible to produce and select layouts which may breathe life into a particular month. Let utilize the entire month of december for instance. December is closely connected with winter and christmas. If we were to make a cricut calendar depending on the month of december, then you will need to pick designs that could mirror this season.

Some fantastic layouts for this month contain reindeers, snowmen, along with santa clause himself. That is so cool would not you say?

In addition to some calendar, the cricut cutting tool may also be utilised to produce your personal gift cards. When you visit malls or to shop that concentrate on selling cards, i'm pretty much certain you'll always be longing for another layout. With the usage of cricut machine together with the attempts from the cricut style studio, then you may produce your gift card with your design and nobody will end you. You're your own boss.

So all these are a few of the most frequent cricut tips which you are able to resort to this will help optimize using your chosen machine. Should you know about several other ways besides that which was just handled, you're free to apply it. It's a free world after all.

Cricut lite cartridges

If you're a craft enthusiast, so you've probably already heard of cricut lite cartridges already. With the rising popularity of garbage reservation, it turns into a remarkably common brand in the world of crafts. When it's for industrial purpose or private hobby, then one is certain to be successful in creating an artistic bit through using devices such as cricut lite cartridges.

All these cartridges are made by the cricut system makers.

The principle intention of creating these instruments is to aid artists to generate more innovative and attractive designs within their various projects. Cricut lite capsules have improved a lot after its launch. To begin with there were just simple white and black cartridges. At the moment, tons of multicolored capsules with vibrant graphics can be found on the industry.

Cricut lite cartridges are extremely manageable. Technically, it's created from plastic which accompanies a thick grip - that can be readily inserted in the cricut system's slotmachine. The device will then browse the things added into it in almost no time.

CRICUT LITE SPECIFICATIONS

As using the cartridge dimensions, it's fine enough to deal with almost any cricut apparatus. Each cartridge comprises many different attractive images - many varieties also consist of different celebration and other intriguing themes. Some cartridges supply a brand new typeface quality which works nicely with upper and lowercase characters.

All cartridges have various images that are related to one another. Examples would be the billionaire cartridge which accompanies a luxury automobile, a hat that is complex, and tube along with the carousel cartridge which has ribbons, jugglers, and other circus material which includes it.

Some cartridges can also arrive with a keypad overlay. This

is a really convenient addition since it reveals exactly what one should get ready for the cartridge. It makes images simple to read and also to place along with a computer keyboard or eliminate them later in the event that you would like.

Cricut lite cartridges arrive in remarkable themes. Each theme has its own own collections of symbols along with a brand new typeface in chosen themes. Some popular topics on the market today contain these:

1. Bloom place - this chance has numerous shrub and blossom designs. It's not difficult to use, without providing issues with your own layers. It includes a coloured instruction card that allows you to observe the qualities and layers of every layout. Bloom cartridge cost is currently at $39.99.

2. Meow place - clearly, it is a motif made from cat images. Such as the bloom collection, it's also readily available for the purchase price of $39.99.

3. Varsity letter series - this collection includes a typeface attribute with group of letters that seem like how it's printed onto a varsity student's coat.

4. Botanicals - this chance allows you observe the beauty of nature via its botanical layouts. Comes with uppercase fonts, so it provides a bit of elegance to your house, scrap books, along with other endeavors. Get your personal botanical chance for $38.95.

5. Cupcake wrappers - this chance is created solely for most

of the cake bakers on the market. It has a bundled 50 cupcake wrappers or picture holders which you may pick from and cut your self to work with to maintain your newly baked cupcakes. You're able to buy cupcake wrappers for cost ranging from $30 - $40.

CONSUMER REVIEWS

In general, consumers locate cricut cartridges helpful due to their scrapbooking and other artwork requirements. With a fantastic choice of themes and shapes, an individual can readily locate a suitable cartridge for virtually any event. Buyers and consumers just whine about the costs that looked somewhat too significant.

Cricut Design Studio - 4 Things You Need to Be Aware of Before Purchasing!

The cricut along with cricut expression house cutting machine have come to be an exciting key for any crafter and trash booker's supply cupboard. Together with the machine's capacity to decrease shapes, letters, and figures at the touch of a button, the cricut is a very simple approach to produce scrapbooking pages, exhibit boards, as well as trendy wall art! The cricut manufacturer has made the system much more intriguing and innovative with all the cricut design studio software. This program takes the cricut system to soaring amounts of imagination. The computer software permits you to hook up your cricut to your house computer and make countless new shapes and designs for the device to reduce.

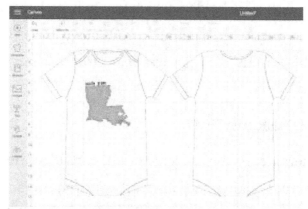

the software comprises a searchable database of each letter, form and amount in the entire cricut cartridge library, so setting tens of thousands of layouts on your palms. And, cricut delivers online upgrades to always increase the library group. Additionally, together with the tools contained, you can get complete control on your own cricut, enabling you to meld (referred welding) letters to a single phrase, and to structure and format objects onto an electronic cutting mat prior to your machine begins its function.

A couple things to keep in mind concerning the cricut design studio software:

1. Although the computer software permits you to see and layout at any cartridge on the market, it's possible to just use the device using all the cartridges you really have. The fantastic thing is that designing distinct things on the pc will provide you a clearer idea about exactly what cartridges you'd like to buy next. Additionally, you may save your layouts for

later usage.

2. Possessing a daily creativity-wise? Want some fresh inspiration? Have a look at the cricut message boards or search the world wide web to look at and get the trendy and imaginative files which additional cricut design studio users've established. This really is a fantastic way to include unique designs to your designs, but additionally to secure fresh and new inspiration.

3. You're able to produce a layout with more than 1 cartridge; you'll simply must have all of the capsules available once you're ready to cutoff.

4. You may still create unique layers to your layouts, such as shadows along with other components. The crucial thing is to make each component on a different layer from the design studio applications to ensure your cricut machine will probably understand to reduce these layers individually and also on the newspaper of your selection.

The cricut design studio software sells for about 6 bucks, and it's a definite must own for any cricut enthusiast. The computer software will loose all your creative thoughts and enlarge the cricut's skills to complete new levels.

Cricut candles - what cricut tote bag works best for the expression machine?

A cricut bag bag is the ideal solution for transporting as well as keeping your cricut machine in your home when you aren't using it. The bags may likewise be employed to keep various accessories such as your capsules and toolkit. The cricut bags generally provide foam cushioning to secure your machine and other pockets for lots of the tools which you may need.

The bigger cricut expression machine is occasionally regarded as the system which shouldn't be carted around. A cricut tote may be utilized to keep the machine in your home, but a lot of croppers prefer to be on the move and visit plants. Bringing their equipment along is essential, therefore you can find now totes which are made large enough to specifically deal with the expression machine. If you're searching for a cricut tote to your own multiplier, ensure the bag is big enough to take care of the larger machine. Tote descriptions especially mention whether the bag is large enough to your expression machine.

One popular storage bag for your expression is a retractable rolling tote. Velcro straps and a solid bottom provide strength and additional reinforcement so the tote can manage the larger expression. The wheels are powerful and the grip makes it effortless to pull alongside you personally. The additional handle makes it feasible to carry them with no usage of these wheels. The interesting part about those bags is that there are various ones out there in trendy colours.

Another option that's readily available for your expression is really a cricut shoulder bag. Picture a massive sport tote and you get a fantastic idea what this bag resembles. It's water proof, and it can be important if transporting an electric appliance. This bag makes carrying out the cricut and additional capsules a breeze since it's extremely roomy. The cushioned and flexible shoulder strap makes the bag comfortable to take. It's also offered in various colors so search about for the colour you want.

A guide to cricut printers and cricut cartridges

Cricut is a renowned brand of server drifting everywhere in the nation. It's an exciting and one of a kind gadget utilized by several people who wish to create creative and excellent projects. As of now, there are 3 unique versions of cricut: the cricut generate machine, luxury cricut expression and needless to say, the foundation version cricut personal electronic cutter machine.

Before improving about that which cricut can give rise to the society, so let us look during its short history. Cricut was initially made by a sizable firm named provo craft that was a little shop. About forty decades back, the organization of provo craft began as a retail shop in the little city of provo, utah. Together with their resourcefulness and imagination, the business eventually expanded after the number of decades. Now, they finally have a total of ten shops with up to 200,000 foot distribution centre.

If you take a close examine the standard cricut machine, so it looks like the visual appeal of a inkjet printer. But it doesn't require a computer to be worked in any way. Even a mean individual may use its purpose as you don't require programming abilities too. Among its advantages include being lightweight. Its blade may also cut thin and thick newspapers that range from 1 inch and 5.5 inches in height.

Cricut only weighs half pounds and that has the power adapter . Additional it's possible to even make it everywhere such as celebration gatherings or event demonstrations because it's a portable item. Using its distinctive and sleek layout, it'll always seem compatible for any crafting office.

As mentioned previously, it could cut to 5.5 inches but that is only one attribute it comprises. It may cut boundaries and names up to eleven inches , therefore, which makes it an ideal match to a newspaper using a measurement of 12x12 inches. Unlike other manufacturers, cricut's key aspect is having the capability to reduce a great deal of stuff. Cricut can also cut a newspaper which has a vast assortment of around 0.5 mm thick. Fortunately, provo craft has supplied additional materials like designer paper pads along with cardstock pads which may be utilized along with cricut cartridges. In reality, these two unique kinds of newspapers are created to have an ideal match with cricut.

Even in the event you ask a lot of users of cricut, then they'd definitely state that cricut digital thermometer is the best one of the top cutters. This is only because cricut cartridges possess a huge selection of choices with respect to styles, fonts and designs, therefore, promoting the maximum degree of imagination without the necessity of a pc.

If you really do not understand using cricut cartridges, they're miniature folds which you put within the cricut for one to place the type of shape, design, font or layout which you would like to cuton. The cartridge even has distinct classes. It comprises: ribbon cartridges, accredited cartridges, form capsules, options capsules and classmate cartridges.

Finally, you're extremely lucky since purchasing a cricut cutter also allows one to get a free cartridge! This totally free cartridge includes some basic shapes which could already provide you the chance to make several shapes and decoration. If not happy, you can purchase additional cricut capsules to add up for your collection. The more chances you have, the greater odds of producing unique artworks.

CHAPTER TWO
USES OF CRICUT MACHINE

Cricut Machine Basics

The cricut machine is leading to a revolution in paper crafting. It's readily portable and operates without being hooked on a computer so that you only pick this up from the handy carrying handle and proceed. But do not allow the advantage fool you, this system isn't a toy. It's capable of producing an unlimited range of letters, shapes, and phrases anything you can imagine. There are no limitations!

The scrapbooking community is mad about the cricut. It's been a celebrity at tens of thousands of "plants" nationally. The testimonials this machine receives from happy clients are remarkable: "beats the contest hands down"; "i am happy I bought the cricut along with my entire family is loving it"; "teacher's best friend!" ; and "the cricut is fantastic - a fantastic tool to own" are only a couple of the magnificent reviews from amazon buyers.

The cricut machine may generate reductions 1" - 5.5" high and around 11.5" long. There are many cartridges accessible to enlarge the cutting edge choices and stress dials that permit the usage of different varieties of paper.

If you wish to go larger, the most recent addition to this cricut cutting platform is your cricut expression 24" personal electronic cutter. It's two brand new cutting mats that measure 12" x 24" and 12" x 12", that lets you reduce characters out of 0.25" up to an astonishing 23.5"

Six new styles along with a number of new functions provide better customization of reductions, and new configurations permit various components of languages and dimensions. The cricut expression additionally comes with an lcd display that shows just what you are looking for another clip. This significant machine is stuffed with features which make it ideal for your classroom or home enterprise.

Last but surely not least is your cricut produce which combines the durability of their first cricut machine together with the performance of this cricut expression device. The cricut drive machine is smaller just like the first cricut system, but lets cuts out of 0.25" around 11.5" onto a 6" x 12" cutting mat also packs at all the characteristics of this cricut expression such as an eight-way vertical blade, portrait style (to cut off pictures), fit to page style (to reduce the most significant cut potential), auto fill mode (to mass create cuts), center point purpose, and twist function. Additionally, it has a better screen screen and slick design.

Cricut additionally carries all you want to finish your jobs: capsules which contain complete ribbon and contour collections, cutting boards, cutting blades, paper-shaping gear, along with a storage bag.

So What exactly are you waiting for? Obtain a Cricut and make creative!

Which Cricut Machine Should you Purchase?

There are 3 versions of this Cricut system, popular private die cutters produced available by the Provo Craft business. With three great possibilities, it can be hard to choose which to purchase. In the event you start little and purchase the first Personal Electronics Cutter? Or is your Expression model value the additional investment? How can the Generate, the hybrid version now being exclusively offered by Michael's Craft Store, stand against both of the other machines?

In numerous ways, all 3 die cut machines will be precisely the same:

All three versions are cartridge-based.

You can only create cutouts depending upon the capsules you possess. Each cartridge includes a computer keyboard overlay, which can be employed in choosing special cuts. The cartridges aren't machine-specific - they may be utilised in any of those 3 versions.

Fundamental performance of three machines is exactly the exact same.

If you have the personal electronic cutter, then you'll not have any trouble working on the cricut expression or produce (along with vice-versa). Why? The fundamental operation of three die cutters would be exactly the exact same.

Here is a fast rundown of this procedure. After plugging in the chosen cartridge and accompanying computer keyboard overlay and turning to the machine, then you're prepared to begin making die cuts. Materials, like paper or cardstock, are set on a particular cutting edge mat, which is subsequently loaded to the machine using all the press of a switch. With another press on this button, the chosen design is selected. All that is left is to choose"cut". The device does the remainder of the job.

All three cricut machine versions utilize the very same accessories.

It was mentioned that the capsules aren't machine-specific, but in addition, this is true with the majority of the additional accessories. It isn't important which version you have - that the replacement blades, blades, different instruments, like the cricut spatula, and design studio applications, may be utilized with almost any version. The 1 exception is that the cutting mats. The machines take various sizes of their mats, and you need to get one that's compatible with your particular machine.

Now that you understand the way the cricut machines are alike, you're most likely wondering how they're different. They change in many ways:

The dimensions of die cuts made by every machine are distinct.

The personal electronic cutter has the capacity of earning cutouts ranging from 1 inch to 5-1/2 inches in dimension, in half inch increments. The generate can create die cuts that range from 1/4 inch to 11-1/2 inches in dimension, per inch inch increments. The expression provides users the maximum flexibility, making cutouts out of 1/4 inch to 23-1/2 inches in dimension, per quarter inch increments.

They size and weight of these machines change.

The personal electronic cutter and produce are equally small, mobile machines. These versions are great for crafters who prefer to shoot their jobs on the street, and make record layouts and other jobs in class settings. They're also suited for people who don't own a particular place in their house place aside for crafting, since these die cutters are easy to package up and set away between applications. The expression, on the other hand, is considerably heavier and bigger. In case you've got a crafting corner or room, and don't have the worries of transferring it regularly, it is a fantastic option.

The three cricut machine versions have various functions and modes.

There are many distinct modes and purposes. By way of instance, the match to page style will automatically correct the dimensions of this die cut predicated upon the dimensions of this material loaded from the system. The middle point function lets you align with the cutting blade across the middle of this substance, so the cut is created about it. The expression machine gets the most flexibility so much as the access to functions and modes. Next in line would be the produce, and third place belongs to the personal electronic cutter. More info could be found regarding such functions and modes in the system handbooks, which can be found in pdf format on cricut.com.

The cost differs for every version.

The personal electronic cutter is the most inexpensive cricut cutter, having an estimated retail price of $299.99. The generate is $100.00 longer, at $399.99, as well as the rake is $499.99. Please be aware that all 3 machines can be bought at substantial savings. Many retailers operate particular sales or possess a lesser regular cost compared to suggested retail cost. It is a fantastic idea to look around when purchasing your very first cricut machine.

Cricut Machine - Beyond the Scrapbook World

Now most men and women feel the cricut system is only just for producing layouts for scrapbooks. They're extremely wrong when they believe like that. This instrument has helped not just scatter bookers but also manufacturers of cards too. Yes, you heard me when I said present cards. The cricut cutting machine is obviously normally created for the newcomer to sophisticated scrap booker.

This poor boy is accountable for cutting newspapers and other substances into the plan or pattern you would like. The plan or pattern could be gotten with the assistance of tools. There's a really famous software tool on the market known as the cricut circuit design studio that has a great deal of layouts that are jazzy. The very best aspect of the software tool is the fact that it allows you to edit the layout they already possess set up and when new layouts can be found, it is possible to upgrade it. That's really cool! Cartridges also come packed with a great deal of layouts which you might also pick from.

The cricut system as mentioned previously could be utilized to earn cards. I am sure everybody has this horrible experience before of becoming frustrated because the shop that you have didn't have the layout that you desired. It can induce great deal of anxiety facing that reality particularly when the individual who you need to provide the card is quite unique. With the support of this cricut design studio, a pc, along with your cricut cutting machine, then you can think of the layout that you need to your own card and ensure that special someone happy. Besides greeting cards, that instrument may also be utilized to produce hangings for partitions, along with calendars.

If you consider anything else which you could do using all the cricut machine, don't hesitate to apply it. There are not any limitations to what you could do.

If you opt to buy one, and that I truly advocate, you will need to spend $300 or more. If this sounds a little too tight for you, you may always start looking for a fantastic bargain on a cricut machine. Look out for earnings on the regional mall or attempt to buy online from ebay or amazon. But keep in mind you don't necessarily have to choose something that's brand new. If you know somebody which has a second hand device however remains in pristine condition, do it. You have to be a smart buyer and spender in precisely the exact same moment.

Joyful cricut searching!

Marsha brasher was crafting for several decades. She loves the challenge of producing cutting documents, and that she understands what is needed to make handmade crafts having the most complex of designs.

Five Strategies For Buying Secondhand Cricut Machine

If you're thinking about purchasing a secondhand cricut device to conserve cash, you're in luck. Since scrapbookers and paper crafters update and purchase newer versions, you will find lots of older versions which are offered for sale on web sites including eBay and craigslist. Oftentimes, these old versions are in great condition, and may be gotten for a fraction of the price of purchasing brand new, a thrifty deal for those seeking to spend less in these challenging financial times.

But, until you plunk down your hard-won money to get a secondhand cricut machine, then there are a couple of things which you ought to ask the vendor to be certain you are in fact getting a fantastic deal:

1. Does the machine have some known flaws?

Even in case the product description doesn't say the occurrence of flaws, it's a fantastic idea to acquire direct confirmation from the vendor. When asked directly, the vendor might tend to completely disclose the state of the machine.

2. Is the vendor willing to offer a short-term guarantee?

If the vendor asserts the system is in great working condition, learn if they'd be eager to deliver a short-term guarantee, for example you for fourteen days. This demonstrates that the vendor is ready to stand behind their merchandise, and provides you with the chance to test out it to confirm it is really defect-free.

3. What accessories are included with this machine?

Locate out what accessories are all included, and also the status of these accessories. By way of instance, if you obtain the cricut personal electronic cutter brand new in the shop, the subsequent add-ons will be comprised: George cartridge, cutting mat, cutting on blade and housing, cable, usb cable, and documentation. If these things aren't included, the price of replacing them must be factored to a complete cost.

4. What are the delivery costs?

If you're buying a secondhand cricut device from a local vendor, this might not be an issue. But in the event the vendor is sending the machine for you, ensure the transport and handling prices are fair and reasonably priced.

5. Will the vendor supply shipping insurance?

Shipping insurance is relatively cheap, but for a commodity like this that may possibly be broken in the delivery process, it's very good practice to get the carrier assistance, like the post office, ups, and fed ex, supply protection, in the event the merchandise is damaged during transport.

Closing ideas...

Purchasing a secondhand cricut system may be a terrific way to spend less. Provided that you've got an open line of communication with the vendor, and also take the essential actions to secure your investment, then you need to not have any issue.

Affordable Cricut Machines - It's All About eBay

Scrapbooking wasn't a simple procedure back as it was still in its baby years. The true procedure was so dull and meticulous that a little mistake was sufficient to allow you to go mad because you needed to begin all over again. However, with the advent of engineering, things have come to be so much simpler and much more convenient. Now, we've got the cricut machine that is mostly responsible for creating scrapbooking so far simpler than it had been 50 decades back.

For the ones that are somewhat interested in what this gadget is, even the cricut gear is a house die cutting instrument. It's effective at providing patterns to newspaper, cloth, and vinyl sheets. The layouts are saved on cartridges that could be retrieved by means of a computer which has a usb. Now is not that cool? Therefore, if you're really considering getting into the practice of scrapbook creating, the cricut system is a tool which you must possess. But keep in mind, this is sometimes an expensive investment. But if you know where to look then it's possible to acquire affordable cricut machines.

A new cricut gear can cost you more than 300. For the fiscally competent, this is no biggie. However, if you're working at minimum wage and have children to send to college and let you pay, this is sometimes considerable investment. The ideal spot to start looking for affordable cricut machines would be to eBay. Ebay is a website where online vendors meet and market their products. In case you go into http://www.ebay.com and enter cricut machines from this search box, then you'll find a large number of outcomes.

The fantastic thing about ebay is that you have the product

right from the vendor rather than via some channel of supply. That is 1 reason many products being offered on ebay are substantially less costly than what you find about the stores or stalls . Exercise precaution since there may be online vendors who are hacks. 1 fantastic method to inspect the profile of this vendor is to receive their feedback score. A feedback score is the evaluation given by individuals whom the vendor has completed business with. Always target for your 99.9 to 100% feedback score or rating.

On EBay you'll get a blend of used and new economical cricut machines. Bear in mind, new isn't necessarily excellent. There may higher versions of some cricut equipment which isn't so old but can be bought in precisely the exact same cost of a lower end product that's brand new. Proceed for the prior. As a scrapbook manufacturer, it's always clear that you would like to have the highest high quality tool. However, in addition, you ought to be sensible and wise. Enough was said.

Get Creative With All the Cricut Machine - 6 Best Suggestions For The Cricut!

Produce Your Handmade Greeting Cards

Have you gone to a shop to get a greeting card? Additionally, it doesn't matter which kind of card it's birthday, Christmas, Easter or only a favorable thinking of one card to ship off to some long lost buddy, you end up turning it on to observe the purchase price. Generally the cost for only one charge card is around $4.00. That's quite pricey for a very simple card.

Why not rather create your own handmade greeting cards along with your cricut machine and also spare the cash whilst making your personal designs? There are several distinct cartridges for several fun layouts. Get creative, vibrant and motivated while creating these cards.

Produce your very own seasonal decorations

Any holiday or season it's simple to think of a number of your holiday decorations with nothing over cricut machines and scrapbooking supplies. Just envision the Christmas trees, valentine hearts or halloween ghosts you are able to possibly make.

Produce your wall decoration

Why spend hours your self or worse yet selecting a muralist to hand painting your favorite letters onto your own walls. You are able to easily do yourself using vinyl die cuts that can produce the exact same appearance as an expert.

Make your die cut decals

Making your die cut decals are a good way to utilize your cricut device. Die cut decals are a terrific present for young kids who just like to stick them anywhere. You are able to use these to make interesting and vibrant posters, school jobs or even to place in decal books. These decals can be reached in any form possible and are much less expensive as going out and buying them at a craft shop.

Creative scrapbooking ideas

Have a kid or expecting soon? Why don't you produce a scrapbook full of their lifestyle! You are able to begin with the day of the arrival and also keep adding pictures as they grow old. If your kid gets older, it is going to be the ideal present (the narrative of the lifetime).

Party or wedding favors

Use with the tags, bags, boxes and much more cartridge to generate party favor creations simple. You may earn anything out of hats, gifts, bags, banner ads or alternative inventions tailored for your precise celebration or wedding motif and colour.

All these are some tips which you may use to make interesting projects together with your defeatist machine. Learn more about the world wide web to discover even more thoughts. Let your creativity go crazy.

Utilize your cricut machine to generate money scrapbooking

If you're into scrapbooking whatsoever no doubt you've learned about provo craft's cricut cutting machines. They're amazing machines which take a good deal of work from tons of jobs, they do not call for a computer to utilize, and they're so straightforward and intuitive to understand much we could know them! If you have used then you most likely have seen just how much fun they could be, but have you ever wondered how to earn money doing what you really love?

Making cash out of the fire is really a dream of most, however they often think that it's too difficult and give up. The fact remains that doing so is not all that hard! The only limitation is the creativity and that which it's possible to create. Here's a few tips to get you started with wondering how to earn some cash with your hobby:

Decorate themed parties

Children like to have themed celebrations. When it's a pokemon celebration, a bakugan birthday celebration, a disney character costume party, children just love them. You might easily earn some cash by creating decoration packs for these sorts of occasions. Print and cut out a lot of different sized decorations, so create customized title tags the children can stick , make playing cards or even personality cards that the children can collect and exchange with one another.

Custom cards and invitations

Who does not adore a personalized thank you card or invitation? It demonstrates that many of love and thought has gone into them. Should you love doing so, why don't you sell some of the creations to produce a little cash at precisely the exact same moment? It's actually surprising how a lot of folks would really like to get a custom made card or invitation created because of their birthdays, birthdays, get-togethers, along with exceptional occasions. Fairly often you neighborhood arts and crafts shop will likewise be inclined to set your creations on display and also market them for their clients. Obviously, they frequently have a cut, but it also saves you the time of needing to go outside and find individuals.

Custom scrapbook layouts

Scrapbooking can edge on an obsession with us. We are constantly trying to create that ideal page design, or locate that perfect touch which can make our scrapbooks that better. You can use the cricut system to create expire cuts of scrapbook page designs and then sell them to other fans on your own. If it's your passion then it'll not be any difficulty coming up with a few to-die-for layouts!

Make a site

You can consistently sell your items online. Nowadays it's really simple to generate a web site. Proceed to blogger.com and register to get a free site, then having just a little practice it's possible to produce a wonderful little site featuring all of the wonderful products that you offer. Place it onto a business card (also free with tons of these online offers on the market) and move it out to anyone that you meet. They are easily able to see all you provide in 1 location and place an order.

All these are only a couple of suggestions for you to begin

making cash with your hobbies. Do not hesitate and believe you're not great enough or it's too hard. Just begin wanting, and you might end up amazed at how great your attempts turn out.

CHAPTER THREE
TYPES OF CRICUT

Cricut Cartridges - Forms and Programs With Cricut Machines

Cricut cartridges are mainly the core of a cricut cutting edge machine, which can be put within the cutter system to form the layout as the consumer wants into a bit of paper.

A wide selection of cartridges can be found on the market all around the earth, although not each one these cartridges operate with all sorts of machines. As an example, the cricut cartridge operates with cricut machines just, and it's the vital element whereby crafters and musicians can create many designs in lovely colors and fashions.

With the fluctuations in printing technologies, a selection of cartridges are introduced recently with more packages to pick from compared to prior ones. The two primary sorts of printer cartridges accessible are: that the ink (utilized from the ink-jet printer)laser cartridges are utilized in laser printers. In the instance of all cricut machines, they still utilize ink-jet printers just.

All roughly cricut ink cartridges:

In the start, cricut ink cartridges were just available in dark, however after some time, a few different colors were released. Afterwards, together with advancement in printing technology, ink cartridges have been created, and attempts have been made to present different font styles, layout and colors for forming contours, too.

The key to success of this cricut system, is the usage of different and special kinds of cartridges that empower users to acquire cut and creative in almost any font, layout, color and fashion.

The general types of cricut cartridges are:

* font cartridge: it includes full alphabets, numbers and other symbols together with font styles as well as other font organizing contours. A few of the favorite all-year seasonal and around cartridges comprise little young, jasmine, teardrop, lyrical characters, pumpkin carving for Halloween, thanksgiving holiday, winter wonderland for your Christmas season, etc.,.

* shape cartridge: it includes many different shapes including boxes, tags and bags, animal, sports, newspaper dolls etc..

* licensed cartridge: it enables users to acquire the cut made with favorite figures such as Disney's micky mouse, hello kitty, pixar toy story, etc..

* classmate cartridge: as its name implies, is specifically

created for classroom functions, which includes classroom fonts, shapesand classroom layout, visual analysis program, suggestions and expressions of educators, etc..

* solutions cartridge: it costs less than the remainder. The contours include welding, baseball, soccer, campout, etc..

The broad collection of cricut cartridges, also as mentioned above, provide crafters, particularly young consumers, an opportunity to experiment with their artistic skills without the support of a computer, whereas the cricut ink cartridge which makes it simpler for them to create designs in a variety of shapes and colors.

Selecting The Ideal Cricut For You

Before you buy your very first cricut, it is important to think about all probable alternatives to decide on the very best machine to match your crafting needs.

First, you must stock up to the fundamentals, such as cricut ribbon and picture capsules. These capsules can come in a variety of topics to showcase and commemorate any event, like holidays, holidays or forthcoming events. You'll also require a huge quantity of coloured paper and a pad on which to reduce that contrasts to the dimensions of your system.

If you're an avid scrapbooker, then you ought to check into buying a first cricut cutter or even the cricut expression. This system will cut shapes, letters and themes to decorate your videos. You might even decorate bulletin boards, posters, party decorations, greeting cards or invitations of any sort. The cutters can also reduce cloth too. It's encouraged that you starch that the cloth first so as to generate the project as simple as possible to your system to finish. The gap between both is straightforward. The cricut 12 is a brand new, 12" x 24" version of the first cricut. This system makes it easier to make large-scale jobs at a sizable quantity - should you've got the right quantity of paper. Font and picture cartridges may be utilized in the two machines.

Have you heard of this cricut cake? This useful product is designed to cut nearly anything for baked products, such as frosting sheets, gum paste, fondant, cookie dough, tortillas, baking soda, chewing gum and the majority of other soft foods substances. Whatever material you choose to use must be involving 1/16" and also 1/8" thick. Maintain the blade clean constantly so as to make sure the very best cut possible.

Another favorite cricut alternative is your cricut cuttle bug. This system is modest. It merely cuts paper that's 6 inches wide and weighs just 7 lbs. The cuttlebug is mainly useful for cutting and embossing particular crafts. This really is the best method to decorate several greeting cards invitations. Once you include a selection of colored expires, then the cuttlebug is going to be prepared to emboss straight away. These dies will also be harmonious with sizzix, big shot and thin cuts machines, that serve a similar function.

Why are you curious and creating your personal t-shirts

and cloth designs? Cricut also created the Yudu for all those crafters that love screen-printing and producing their own layouts. The Yudu enables its owners to attach to some laser ink jet printer and generate a layout to screen-print onto virtually anything! Yudus are used for straps, handbags, photograph frames, and shoes - you name it.

Finally, in the event you would like to nourish your newfound cricut obsession, then go right ahead and buy one of those newest cricut gypsys. This useful, hand-held apparatus will keep your ribbon cartridges for simple portable usage. You're able to design from anyplace on the move, in the physician's office, even while on holiday, or merely sitting on your sofa. Anything you plan onto the gypsy is totally transferable to a cricut device for cutting edge. Should you save your layout, it may be linked to some of your cricut apparatus and published at a later moment.

This is a succinct overview of a number of the cutting edge machines cricut presently sells. Because you can see there's a fantastic assortment of machines to get whichever specific kind of craft that you wish to concentrate on. 1 thing is for certain. Whichever machine you select you will have many hours of inspiration and fun producing and creating your own crafting projects.

Although, apparently all of the versions of cricut cutting machines operate in a similar method to some extent using a little bit of variation on precisely the exact same design and characteristics, the cricut design has emerged as a versatile system which has changed the crafting sector by introducing a few new features that improve its functionality.

The cricut machine empowers users to reduce different letters, shapes and phrases in to fine dimensions such as classroom décor, signage, scrapbooks, and much more.

Characteristics Of Cricut Expression machine:

- it's quite simple to work with.

- The Cricut Expression Cartridge does not require a computer as it includes Plantin School Book and Accent Essentials.

- The whole library of present Cricut Cartridge may be utilized.

- It empowers users to decrease figures from 1/4 inches from dimension to around thrilling 11-1/2 inches.

- It includes LCD display that's easy to see and reveals precisely what's being typed.

- Cut landscape and portrait dimensions.

- The program supplies a number mode to pick the amount of cuts that the consumer needs of these chosen on the screen.

- The auto-fill manner can help to fill pages using as many characters as will fit on the specific page.

- By employing this Cricut Expression Cartridge present library that the user may utilize a vast selection of creative attributes in precisely the exact same cut according to choice.

- The built in paper saver mode can help you to occupy the smallest amount of space possible in the newspaper.

- The line-return work will help to acquire precise spacing by producing line breaks in every single cut.

- Fit-to-length along with fit-to-page works readily set how big the duration of a chosen cut on every page.

- The other side permits users to acquire a flipped-mode picture cut of their selected shape.

- It comes in several distinct languages: French, English, German and Spanish - its produced in China, also has a 90 day guarantee.

What Makes the Cricut Expression Machine Much Better Than The Rest?

There are certain attributes the cricut cutter features that makes it distinct from other Cricut machines:

- It's bigger in dimension than many others.

- Compared with other machines it may cut much bigger designs around 23-1/2 inches in complete, which empowers the user to make banner layouts, too.

- As anticipated, with enhanced attributes, the cutter also comprises a high price tag, too.

Despite all of the gaps together with other existing machines that the fantastic news isit has some resemblance with the old one which makes it increasingly useful. This specific Cricut Machine employs exactly the exact same cartridge as other cutters, so therefore, an individual may update his present Cricut into a new one and utilize his/her assortment of older Cartridges. Even though the Cutter comes with its Cricut Expression Cartridge, undoubtedly, it provides you with additional design choices.

Cricut Scrapbooking Machine Review

If you're an avid scrapbooker, you need to get one of those machines. They're the greatest garbage booking enthusiast's buddy. They operate simply by loading a cartridge to the machine and picking out literally tens of thousands of possibilities for the decorating ideas.

The phrases and also the border may be an incredible 11 1/2 inches . The cartridges you buy on the Cricut scrap washing machine will provide you the choice of picking from over 250 layouts. And that isn't all. The dimensions of these layouts are from 1 inch to 5 1/2 inches.

How a lot of men and women may create their garbage book as beautiful as possible using this superb machine to provide you with professional results each moment? The broad variety of shapes, letters, layouts, and phrases to grow your scrap book will probably help it become a precious book for several years to come.

This is a fantastic gift idea for anybody who loves crap booking. The newspaper slides and everything you do is push a single button. The machine manages the remainder. The portability of this Cricut is yet another notable feature. It weighs just 7 pounds that's excellent for carrying along on a visit from town for a couple of days or into some buddy's home that shares your own hobby.

Another in the household of Cricut products is your Private Electronics Cutter that has exactly the very same dimensions as the standard Cricut machine however, it's the choice of permitting you to cut out of a quarter of a inch up to 11.5 inches. The Personal Electronic Cutter includes a blade which enables cutting edge from eight distinct ways.

The Cuts you are able to make with this particular eight way blade are amongst others these reductions:

Portrait

Fit to page

Auto fill

Center Stage

Flip function

All these features aren't on the normal Cricut cutter. The advancements which were created are great additions like the display screen was improved along with the layout appears to be much skinnier.

Cricut Expressions is a bit larger than the standard Cricut. It wasn't supposed to be portable as the other two; rather it's to remain put to a desk or inside a meeting area. There could be gaps in dimensions and the capability to choose the Cricut Expressions filler with you however all of them use exactly the identical size capsules as well as the very same blades.

When you need letters, numbers, shapes, or whatever else cut to the scrap book or anything you want them the cricut expression is the cutter. The capability to mix and match with the attributes on the very first cut is among the remarkable elements of this machine.

There is no demand to get a computer since everything you'll need is at the cartridge which you load in the machine. An LCD display will show you exactly what directions you're typing in and also the preferences for speech and dimensions are changeable.

If you enjoy scrap booking and wish to obtain all your books so and put up precisely how you would like them to seem, you are going to need to try these Cricut crap booking machines.

That Scrapbooking Machine If You Select?

If you're thinking of getting a cutting edge machine to better your crafting projects, you've probably already discovered there are a vast array of machines from which to pick. How can you select which machine is going to be the right for you? Cost, obviously, is the largest deciding factor, however, where would you go then? Do you desire a manual system or a digital system? Would you wish to get individual expires, cartridges with numerous pictures, or would you desire the extreme flexibility of a pc based system? Listed below are a number of details about the sorts of cutting machines out there.

Manual Die Cutting Machines

Manual Cutting machines need no power and are managed by hand. They're the cheapest of your alternatives. A number of those manual cutters comprise the Cuttlebug, the Sizzix, as well as also the Quickut Squeeze or even the Quickut Revolution. You'll have to acquire individual dies for all these machines, one for each form that you would like to reduce. The Cuttlebug, among the most recent versions of guide cutters, will utilize expires from many manufactures and contains a wonderful embossing attribute. The Cuttlebug along with the Sizzix will reduce pretty thick materials such as chipboard, fun felt and foam. The Sizzix, nevertheless, is among the earliest die cutting machines offered and can be limited to a single or two fonts. Every one these components are mobile for carrying along to plants or holidays.

Digital Cutting Machines

You can choose digital cutting machines which stand alone or those that need the usage of a pc. The Cricut along with the Cricut Expression don't need to be plugged into the pc. These machines utilize cartridges designed especially for all these machines. Each cartridge be bought separately but includes several pictures. There's optional applications available to your Cricut should you would like to enhance the flexibility of those systems.

There are several computer-based versions out there for home usage, such as the Quickz Silhouette, Xyron Wishblade, and Craft Robo. All three of those machines are essentially the same, letting you cut some true type font you've got on your PC. The Wishbone is the most costly of the three, however it will include additional designs and applications. Your layout choices are wide open using one or more of these machines. In case you have problems learning precisely how to run the machine, you will find support groups on the internet where you'll discover seasoned crafters keen to assist. You could even save your layouts on the internet or email them . Needless to say, those machines are more costly than standalone or manual machines.

Which Cutting machine is most suitable for you?

Now you have to decide which cutting edge machine would be the ideal fit for your needs. Do your own research and be truthful with yourself. Just how much are you ready to make investments? How long do you must use your device? Can it be too hard for you to understand the methods for the more complex versions? Will buying person dies or capsules limit your imagination and be more expensive in the future than a larger up front investment? As soon as you answer these questions, then you'll be more prepared to opt for a cutting machine which will best fit your own needs.

With Cricut Cutting Machines On The Craft Projects

More and increasing numbers of folks are deciding to create their own scrapbooking stuff, invitations and cards. These do-it-yourself choices allow considerably more room for customization compared to their mass produced choices. Not just are homemade invitations much more customizable, but they also cost much less than shop - bought options. Circut private cutting machines also make it feasible for those who have minimal time and much less expertise to create professional looking craft jobs anytime.

Cricut Cutting machines can be found anyplace in craft shops in addition to some department stores which contain craft and art segments. On the other hand, the very best prices are usually located on the internet. For your occasional do-ityourselfer, the entry level version, with easily available sale costs of about $100 is more than adequate. It's more than capable of generating a huge number of distinct shape mixes and requires very little maintenance. More seasoned crafters, or people who handle home companies that produce personalized paper products, might discover that bigger versions are more in accordance with their demands.

All these machines are semi automatic, and much simpler to use than manual paper cutters. Typically, they could cut through very heavy paper stock, allowing scrapbookers to make designs with many different shades and textures. For advice about the best way best to use a machine, there are a range of websites offering information from frequent amateur customers. They may be an important source of the inspiration and information, showing the way the machine might be best employed. When these websites are a terrific destination for people that are only beginning, the very best feature of a house Cricut machine would be your capability to make completely one-of-a-kind webpages. Experiment with new form and colour combinations to make something distinctive and memorable.

Cricut Cutting Machines Are Flexible Enough For Use For Any Type Of Craft Job.

Make professional searching scrapbooks using Circut Personal Cutting Machines

A cricut cutting machine is essential have for any scrapbooker. These machines make it possible for consumers to cut paper to some range of intriguing contours, making personalizing each page at a scrapbook simple and enjoyable. Made to be modest enough to bring with you once you travel, they'll occupy little space in your house and may be carried with you to get almost any scrapbooking celebrations you might attend. They're the ideal tool for everybody who's searching for a user friendly way of producing unique boundaries, inserts or alternative page vases.

Cricut machines can produce shapes which are anywhere from 1" to over just 5" tall. Simple to alter metal cutting patterns have been utilized to make uniform contours in many kinds of craft paper. These forms may be used to include custom decoration, festive contours or intriguing boundaries that can reflect the information of every webpage. As many distinct thicknesses of card stock might be used, scrapbookers ought to be conscious that paper at a milder grade might cause the blades to boring faster. This usually means that you should constantly keep a tab on the sharpness of the blade and then replace them if needed to keep great outcomes.

A cricut machine isn't a little investment. Prices begin at about $100 online, which might put this cutting edge machine from reach for a few. But when taking into consideration the price of buying packs of pre-cut shapes and letters, most dedicated scrapbook fans do discover the system will eventually pay for itself. In addition, it can be utilized for additional newspaper based crafts, like making custom invitations, gift tags and cards. The cricut firm has a good reputation in the trading globe, and their products are know to be durable, therefore no replacement ought to be required, in spite of heavy usage.

Searching For Your Cricut Accent Essentials Cartridge?

The cricut accent essentials is among these die cut capsules which everybody wants. But it can be tough to find since it's sold exclusively using all the expression machine. If you don't have the expression, or if you bought a cricut system which didn't incorporate this particular cartridge, there's very good news if it's in your record of must-haves. For those who know where to look, you can purchase this, and in a pretty decent cost! Or, if you're particularly thrifty, you might even have the ability to get it at no cost. Continue reading to learn just how...

1. Create a trade.

If you truly need the accent essentials cartridge, but don't wish to cover this, you might have the ability to exercise a transaction, either temporary or permanent, together with somebody who possesses this particular cartridge. If you frequently attend plants or have a set of record buddies you want to meet up , inquire to see whether anybody will be inclined to figure out a transaction.

Many scrapbookers also see forums and other internet

places, like sites, to go over their own projects. Join a discussion and render an easy article, detailing exactly what cartridges you'd be ready to part with to be able to work out a market. Forums and sites are fantastic places to place this kind of petition, due to the amount of individuals seeing these online meeting areas. You could be amazed by the amount of answers you get.

2. Have a look at classified advertising.

You can take a look at your regional classified ads to determine if anybody has the product you would like listed available. Even better however, extend your search to internet classified listings to find out if anybody has got the cartridge available on the market. Craigslist along with other similar sites make it possible for users to post things they wish to sell. Unlike neighborhood classified listings, several internet vendors don't have any trouble sending things to buyers which don't reside within their regional area.

3. Visit online stores.

Even though cricut doesn't market the accent essentials cartridge separately, and you won't have the ability to discover it in retail shops, online shoppers have additional options. Several internet retailers swap out the capsules contained with machines so as to personalize orders to their clients. Because of swapping, a number of these online shops have this distinctive cartridge readily available for sale.

4. Assess online auctions.

Online auction websites, like ebay, are also excellent places to search down hard-to-find products. Many buyers can pick up things for a fraction of the price.

As you are able to see, that the cricut accent essentials cartridge really isn't really that hard to discover. Whether you're seeking to produce a transaction or to buy it, then you need to not have any trouble finding it in a cost you prepared to cover.

CHAPTER FOUR
HOW TO START CRICUT

The Cricut Machine

The Cricut system is a really renowned invention. It's helped scrapbookers and lots of individuals with their demands not just restricted in the scrapbook creating planet but also to other aspects too. It's to be mentioned however that the 1 sector it's helped is on the scrapbooking kingdom. From the fantastic old dark ages, even if you weren't proficient at carvings or in case you didn't understand how to compose, your favorite moment goes down the drain.

Those two would be the sole means of maintaining the memories back afterward. It might appear crude and ancient to us back then, it was that they needed. Now, we've got everything set up to the preservation of someone's memories and also we all to Father Technology.

When a scrapbooker makes the decision to make a scrapbook, that the layout is almost always a key consideration. Before, picking a design can cause migraines of epic proportions but today is another story. The cricut system to be mentioned is only accountable for cutting edge newspapers, vinyl, and cloth according to a particular pattern or layout. The design or pattern can be made or edited by means of a software application known as the Cricut Design Studio.

If you're searching for simple and well - recognized designs which are already built - in, you proceed for capsules that are secondhand. There's not any limitation to everything you could think of using the layouts which are already set up. The golden rule would be to allow your creativity go crazy. This really is a tool which any aspiring scrapbooker must possess. So far is it? The prices generally start at $299 and will go up based on the version which you pick.

It might appear to be substantial sum of money however, the expense is well worth it. But if you wish to employ the additional effort to learn to locate a fantastic deal, you're more than welcome about this. The world wide web is almost always a wonderful place to get some excellent bargains, you simply have to look. There is Amazon, eBay, so a lot more.

The cricut machine has lots of uses besides being a cutter of layouts to get a scrapbook. The layouts itself may be used to make different things like greeting cards, wall decorations, and more. You simply have to believe creatively. There are not any limitations and when there are, they're only a figment of your own imagination.

The Cricut Machine - A Short and Intimate Appearance

When you think about building a scrapbook, the very first

thing comes in your head is exactly what pictures to put. That is fairly simple as all you want to do would be to pick images that highlight a particular event or happening on your lifetime. After this was completed, at this point you should think of the layout to the scrapbook. Again, this can be quite simple as everything that you have to do is base your choice on whatever occasion has been depicted on your own pictures. Let us take for instance, a wedding day.

Pick a design which will transfer that audience back in time and relive everything transpired throughout your wedding day. Common sense is everything you may need here. The next thing is to produce the layout. How can you take action? Can you do it ? No is the reply to those above query. You do so through the usage of a cricut machine.

The cricut machine is a fantastic creation. This poor boy is able to help you cut paper, cloth, and vinyl sheets to whatever pattern you would like. The actual production of these designs may be achieved via software tools like the cricut layout studio or via capsules using pre - engineered designs assembled in to them. Therefore, if you're enthusiastic scrap booker, this system is essential have.

How exactly how does one cost? Well every unit comes with an average cost of $299 with greater versions having larger price tags. However there are means by which you'll be able to find a less expensive price. In case you've got a pc with internet, proceed browse and hunt for great bargains and inexpensive cutting machines that are secondhand. EBay is a good place to begin with.

Recall nevertheless, that carrying purchases through eBay can take dangers so that you need to be certain you check out each of the vendor's profiles which you may want to participate in. If you're the fantastic conventional shopper who'll never devote to internet purchasing, you could do this old - school and then buy from a mall through earnings or anything else similar.

The cricut machine has additionally many applications which extend far beyond the domain of scrapbooking. Given the amount of layouts which might be in your own cartridge or software application, you may always utilize them to make cricut calendars, hangings such as partitions, and greeting cards for special events. Your creativity is the one thing which may limit your creativity.

Marsha Brascher was crafting for several decades. She loves the challenge of producing cutting documents, and that she understands what is needed to make handmade crafts having the most complex of designs.

Cricut Suggestions - Tips That May Help You to Get Started

Capturing memories onto a virtual camera, even an HD camera, and a voice recorder make life much more purposeful. When there's a unique moment which you would like to catch and be in a position to return to at any certain time, you are able to certainly do this so easily with the assistance of these instruments. However, pictures continue to be the favorite medium by the majority of people. If you wish to put together those images and compile them onto a distinctive memorabilia, then you flip into scrapbooking.

Scrapbooking is a technique of preservation of thoughts that's been in existence for quite some time and it's evolved up to now better. Previously, the invention of a single scrapbook was a monumentally crazy job. But now, with the Creation of devices like the Cricut cutting edge machine, matters are made simpler. If you're Looking to Developing a scrapbook, this poor boy is the instrument for you. There Are Lots of good cricut thoughts out there you can make the most of.

Scrapbooks are only some of many cricut thoughts on the market. This instrument, if you understand how to optimize it makes it possible for you to create things which go past scrapbooking for example calendars. If you buy a cricut cartridge, then there are a slew of layouts uploaded in every and every one. All these pre- made themes may be used for a whole lot of items like hangings for partitions, image frames, picture frames, and greeting cards for many seasons.

Just your creativity will limit your advancement using a cricut machine. Together with calendars, you are able to design every month to represent the weather, the disposition, and exceptional events which are connected with that. The cricut machine will take care of this. But in case one cartridge doesn't have the layout that search, you may always go and purchase. It's that simple!

Cricut machines may be a little expensive with all the cost starting at $299. That's pretty hefty for anybody to begin with. Be a smart buyer. You may always turn into the world wide web to seek out great bargains on cricut machines. Purchasing from eBay may also be a terrific move but can take several dangers if you aren't experienced with eBay. In case you're quite worried about this, you always have the option to await a purchase to occur at one of the regional malls and buy out there since it will probably have a guarantee.

Those are among the numerous great cricut thoughts on the market. Calendars so many more could be made with the usage of this machine that is fantastic. Bear in mind, only your imagination will restrict what you could do.

Earning Your Cricut Mat Sticky Again

Are you aware you don't have to obtain a new mat every-time your mat reductions it is stickiness?

When your mat reaches the point at which nothing will adhere and your newspaper only moves around if you attempt to reduce, then it is time to"re-stickify" (is that a phrase??) Your mat. This is a really straightforward procedure and you'll be stunned at how well it's working!

• Step 1- Carry your mat into your sink. Utilize some hot

water, a couple drops of dish soap and a green scotch brite washing machine. Scrub your mat beneath the tepid water. You will begin to find the small pieces of newspaper and filthy sticky grime begin to come off. You might even utilize the scrapper which came on the Cricut tool kit that will assist you scrap away some of the gunk also. Keep scrubbing before all of that additional layer of gunk is eliminated. Based upon your mat, then this can strip it all of the way to the vinyl with no stickiness left or right there can still be a little quantity of stickiness. Either way would be fine.

• Step 2- You then wish to let it airdry or use your own hair dryer. Do not use a towel to wash it since it is going to leave lint .

• Step 3- Permit that airdry for approximately one hour. It is ready to rock & roll up back again. I've done this on my mats and over again.

• Measure 4- Then, have a wide tipped ZIG 2 way glue pen and use paste in lines round the entire mat.

• Measure 5- Permit dry for 1 hour before implementing the translucent sheet back .

Cricut Sale - Enhancing Your Abilities

If a man was great at something, could he do it at no cost? Sometimes, the response will be"yes". However, if it's a skill which you feel can deliver food onto the table you want to capitalize on it. Therefore, in case you've got a cricut cutting tool, a program, and a knack for managing layouts and patterns, then this may be a better opportunity for you to measure and begin earning. This is where it is possible to find a cricut sale.

The cricut machine may be utilized to cut the layouts that you pick from the applications tool. With the support of this cricut style studio, it is possible to eventually discover the layout that you search for a great deal of stuff. However, before we proceed any farther with the idea of ways to acquire a cricut purchase, let's understand the various applications of the designs and patterns which we get out of our applications.

Greeting cards are among the most frequent items that the layouts are utilized for. The cover is easily the most likely recipient of those designs or layouts. Therefore, if you currently have an issue in your mind; plug on your personal computer, activate the program and search for your layout. In case the cover copes with a Christmas motif then search for layout that will tell the story of Christmas. It's that simple. Consequently, if you understand those who desire their gift cards customized, then this is definitely the most opportune time to you allow the company person in you talk.

The production of calendars is an additional fantastic undertaking which you're able to participate in using all the designs and layouts which come from your own software. Utilize the layouts to breathe life to every month using the design/s which you opt for. If we're speaking about December, subsequently select designs which have a Christmas theme for this. Last but not least, yet another one of the most frequent applications of the program patterns and layouts are available on decorations for partitions. There are not any limitations to what you could do this so the essential thing is to simply let your creativity go crazy on the decoration you may produce.

So that you have it. As soon as you master the craft of producing the three which were only mentioned, you'll have a cricut sale very quickly. But naturally, you also will require determination and endurance to produce this work.

Crafting Hobbyists - With the Cricut Machine

Crafting is among the most well-known hobbies in the world these days. You can find many men, women and even kids who like crafting and a few who make a professional living from it. There are tons of unique instruments, gear and software applications available to assist these crafting fans take advantage of their moment.

The cricut machine is merely that. It's a digital cutter which aids with newspaper crafts. With only a touch of a button it is possible to make amazing designs and receive assistance with crafts such as home decor, art, paper crafting and much more. The device is quite simple to navigate and utilize so the one thing that you truly need to be worried about is being imaginative and allowing your imagination run rampant.

There is no demand for a pc to utilize the Cricut device. All you will need is a conventional electric outlet to plug it into and you're prepared to go. Before you begin it's helpful to bring a little bit of time and make more comfortable with the equipment. Have a peek at the newspaper feed to comprehend how everything operates.

The on button, then cut button and stop switch will be grouped with the right of this device, the newspaper feed in the rear.

To begin, first determine what crafts that you wish to perform on. Put a cricut cartridge to the system and you also get to select from various layouts, sizes and receive every detail from the way. There are hundreds and hundreds of possibilities so that the layouts you can produce with your crafting will be infinite.

There is a user manual which is included with the device when you buy it give this a browse through in the event that you're experiencing any issues. The Cricut system is a priceless investment for any crafter who chooses their hobby seriously.

Three Approaches to Boost Your Growing Time

The cricut electronic mail machine paired using all the cricut design studio applications has opened a completely new universe of designing chances for scrapbookers and cardmakers alike. Though a lot people have plenty of materials and tools, the 1 thing we appear to be lacking over every other is the time. It's crucial to utilize the time we can see into the fullest if we would like to finish additional jobs. Here are 3 approaches to make the most of your time creating.

1. Maintain appropriate maintenance on your own machine, mat, blade and gear.

If you spend few added minutes it can take to maintain your system in good shape it will help save you money and time in the long run. The two largest culprits appear to be the blade along with the cutting mat. Change out your blade if needed to prevent from wasting paper with ripped or less-than-perfect cuts and also the time that it requires to re-cut your own images. If you attempt to extend out using your mat also long that the newspapers will start to move and slip as the device cuts. It is more than worthwhile to execute the age old information about doing things correctly the first time.

2. Become knowledgeable about the individuals who may assist you. Getting to be aware of the tools available to assist you may help you save time once you get stuck together with the equipment and applications. The most significant source in my view is your Cricut message boards. There are a few terrific folks on the market more than prepared to answer virtually any question you've got and assist with ideas.

3. Do not reinvent the wheel. If you don't merely delight in playing and designing with the application, there is no reason

to recreate a document somebody else has already produced. There are many sites and websites where other Cricut users discuss the jobs as well as the corresponding documents they've designed.

There is No reason to devote valuable time designing cuttings from scratch if somebody has put it to the net that you utilize. Even when you simply use the foundation of this layout as a starting point for incorporating your own developments, you will still save a whole lot of time rather than attempting to determine how to make the document in the very start. 1 thing to bear in mind is to always give credit where credit is due, even in the event that you decide to alter the document in 1 manner or the other.

Spend a small amount of additional time up front by maintaining your resources at tip-top shape, becoming to understand where to locate assistance, and with other people's layouts as soon as you're able to. If you do, if you sit down to focus on a project you might just realize you have additional time to really finish it than you ever believed.

CHAPTER FIVE
TIPS ON HOW TO GET
STARTED WITH CRICUT

25 Tips & Tricks To Get Cricut Newbies

O k, so a number of these tips and tips are VERY simple, and therefore are for the complete novice to Cricut machines. But be certain to scan through the entire list since we guarantee there is a hint or hint with your title on it!

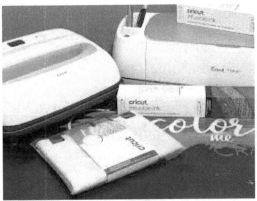

1. Register To Cricut Accessibility

If you really want to get the maximum from owning a Cricut Research Air two, we then advocate subscribing to Cricut Accessibility . It's possible to pay a monthly charge of about $10, or even a yearly fee that proves to be marginally cheaper a month.

Cricut access provides you access to 30,000+ images, 1000's of jobs and more than 370 fonts. If you're likely to use your own Cricut a whole lot, then that can save a great deal of cash than if you should get every undertaking and picture separately.

Plus it is less of a hassle to cover a set rate compared to stressing about just how much cash you are actually spending projects! It provides up! Make your money's worth from your Cricut by creating the amazing Design Space jobs.

2. De-tack Your Cutting Mat

De-tack Your own Cricut cutting mat a bit!

The Explore Air 2 typically includes The green normal cutting mat, although the Maker generally will come with all the grim light clasp mat. You put your stuff on the mat prior to placing it in the machine.

The green cutting mat is fairly tacky when new! Once you peel off the plastic cap off, then you can put a clean, sterile t-shirt within the mat to be able to prime it to your very first job. It is quite tough to acquire that the cardstock off, even in the event that you have all of the resources, when it is in its entire stickiness! It's simple to hurt the project whilst attempting to get off it.

You should not have this issue with the grim light clasp mat, which means you might also buy that for your card and paper jobs rather than de-tacking the mat.

3. Maintain Your Cutting Mat Covers

The cutting mats Include a Plastic shield . This may be pulled away and place back easily.

We maintained our pay and put it back our mat once we are done with this it retains the mat tacky and clean longer!

4. Fixing The Cricut Cutting Mat

Every once and a while (or even every Time you use it), provide your cutting mat a wash over with a few baby wipes.

The non-alcohol water packs without aroma are greatest. This can help keep it free of creating up using cardstock and plastic residue out of cuttingedge, and the normal family dust and lint drifting around.

5. Get The Ideal Tools

It includes a useful instrument, also a scraper, tweezers, a spatula along with scissors. It's particularly beneficial to have the weeding tool if you're considering cutting adhesive plastic or heat transport vinyl.

6. The Cricut Scoring Stylus

So a number of the card jobs ask that you get the scoring stylus. I didn't purchase one with my equipment initially, and thus needed a debilitating wait for it to arrive until I really could go to a better jobs. If you purchased your system as part of a package, it might possess the scoring stylus contained, so double check .

7. Start with The Sample Project

Once your device arrives, begin with The sample job.

The research air two and maker include sample stuff for an initial job. Unless you purchase a Cricut Bundle, you get the minimum number of stuff to do this small thing, however it is ideal to begin simple!

Instead of attempting to do anything big and elaborate, simply start here in order to find a sense of how things work software and hardware wise.

8. Evaluation Cuts

After doing your own jobs it may be sensible to perform a test cut prior to doing the entire thing. If the blade has been set too low it will destroy your cutting mat. When it's too large it might just cut marginally during your vinyl, cardstock, etc. and mess up your materials.

Doing a test trimming may involve asking your system to cut a little circle. Check the atmosphere is correct and make adjustments if needed.

9. Alter Pen Lids After Utilization

It is very important to have the lid it Asap after you have finished using it that it will not dry out. They're too costly to waste. The neat thing about the Design Space jobs is the fact that it frequently prompts one to set the lid back !

10. Aged Cricut Cartridges

Do not forget to hook up any older Cartridges you might have obtained from a former device to your account. This is a rather easy process, as displayed below.

Each chance can simply be connected after, so if you are taking a look at purchasing some second hand, then affirm that this has not been achieved yet!

Besides utilizing the right tools to eliminate your cardstock or plastic in the leading mat, there's just another trick to getting off it.

Rather than peeling your project from the mat, that could lead to curling (or overall mangling), peel away the mat from the undertaking. Bend the mat from the card instead of the other way round.

12. Purchase The Deep Cut Blade

There is nothing worse than placing your heart upon a project and then finding you do not have the ideal tools!

The heavy cut blade lets One to cut deeper leather, card, chipboard and much more. This blade works with all the Explore Air 2. It's necessary to not just get the bladebut the blade casing too.

13. Totally free SVG documents

You do not only have to use layouts in the design space shop. You may either make your SVG documents, or utilize other free SVG documents that may be found all around the world wide web.

14. Alternative Pens For Cricut

You are not stuck just with Cricut Pens in Cricut Machines!

You may use Cricut pencil adapters (such as that 1) so as to utilize any pencil with the Maker or Air Conditioning 2. Look at these Cricut Etsy Finds for much more weird and Terrific inventions for Cricut!

15. Load Mat Correctly

Ensure that your mat is properly filled before you begin cutting. It ought to slide beneath the rollers. Your device will probably just begin cutting ahead of the cap of the grid onto the mat or perhaps not if it has not been loaded directly.

16. Utilize Free Fonts

You will find so many free font websites for one to begin using!

Browse the internet to get a listing of free fonts for Cricut. You only download the fontand install it on your own computer and it'll appear on your Cricut Design Space (see next tip).

Regrettably, among the greatest fonts, Samantha Font, isn't readily available free of charge, however check that connection to learn where you are able to get it to get the very best price!

17. Installing Themes

After installing a ribbon to your computer, you might want to sign up and back to Cricut Design Space prior to your font will appear there. You might even have to restart your pc in order for it to appear (mine would not appear without restarting my pc).

For more information read the way to set up fonts from Cricut Design Space.

18. Fixing Blades

Like that which, Cricut blades utilize out. If the reductions are no more so smooth and powerful it is time for a shift. Other Indicators that you Want a brand new blade comprise:

§ Tearing plastic or card

§ Lifting or pulling off vinyl off the backing sheet

§ Not cutting all of the way through (ensure your trimming setting is right too)

You can buy brand new blades Amazon or see that Cricut Blade Guide for much more purchasing choices.

19. Whenever Your Favorite Looses Its Stick

Cleaning your mat is 1 approach for slightly more life from your cutting mat. However, if it is beyond this, and you haven't purchased a brand new cutting mat still, you may tape off your plastic or card to maintain it in position.

Evidently, you do not need to tape over a place that's having to be trimmed down a few sides must perform the job. Even a moderate tack painters tape is ideal to this undertaking, and ought not to harm your cardstock.

20. Cricut's Custom Cut Settings

The Explore Air two includes 7 preset Choices on the dial:

§ Paper

§ Vinyl

§ Iron-on

§ Light cardstock

§ Cardstock

§ Bonded fabric

§ Poster board

If the material you're cutting is not on this listing, there's a customized option that you'll be able to pick on the dialup. Visit Design Space, choose your project and click'Make It'. Then you will have the ability to choose your content by a drop down menu.

Or you may produce a new custom made cloth. You may find more info relating to it on in Cricut's site .

21. Various Blades For Different Materials

Some Folks swear by using different Blades for cutting every substance.

By way of example, using one blade which you merely use for cardstock, and yet another that you merely use for the vinyl. That is because the a variety of stuff will wear otherwise on your own blades. Cutting plastic is simpler on the blade compared to cutting card.

Having a committed blade to get vinyl means that it will remain sharp and ready, instead of having a blade to get all that immediately goes dull then lifts your vinyl!

22. Mirror Your Pictures For HTV

If you're cutting heat transfer vinyl together with your Cricut, then you'll have to mirror your own design!

Once you choose'Make It' there's a choice to mirror your layout (as seen below), and you'll need to pick this choice for every individual mat!

23. Set HTV The Perfect Way Up

In order to lower heat transport vinyl you'll have to set your vinyl polished side down on the outer mat.

This way the carrier sheet is. Beneath along with the dull plastic side is at the top. It is difficult to determine which side the carrier sheet is around, so remember polished side down and you are going to be OK!

24. Weeding Boxes

If you're cutting a little or intricate layout, or you're cutting a great deal of unique designs on a single sheet of vinyl, so it can help use weeding boxes.

Simply use the square instrument in cricut design room to put a box around your layout and set both components together. Unlock the silhouette at the bottom left corner manipulate it in a rectangle.

This makes weeding easier than weeding several layouts at the same time on the 1 sheet of vinyl, and even simpler than attempting to observe where your layouts are cutting them out individually using scissors.

25. Don't Forget to Establish The Dial

This suggestion sounds like a no brainer; however,how often have I forgotten how to alter the material placing?!

It is this easy thing to overlook -- Particularly once you have finally completed your layout and really wish to get clipping edge! The humorous thing is that Cricut Design Space really tells you exactly what substance that the dial is put into if you're just about to cut a layout -- but it's not difficult to forget that also!

Save the mistake of cutting on Right through to a cutting mat, or perhaps through your cardstock -- check your dialup!

... And today we've a bonus tip!

26! Keep A Source Of Materials

As we mentioned previously, it is a nuisance If you would like to begin a project and you do not have the perfect tools.

As an instance, we have been capable of being with no grading stylus, without the ideal pencil for a job, and with no profound cut blade. However, another hassle is if you would like to do a project and you have run out of glue plastic, HTV or cardstock!

CHAPTER SIX
PRECAUTIONS TO CRICUT MACHINE

Be A Specialist in Locating Affordable Cricut Cartridges

The invention of Cricut machine also has made newspaper crafting a hobby to expire! This system made craftwork easier and more intriguing. It permits you to expire cut shapes and fonts of various sizes from other paper materials in the touch of a button. This system doesn't include affordable Cricut cartridges that are utilized to make your own shapes and fonts.

A Personal Cutter out of Provo Craft will charge you less $299 and also the fancier Cricut Expressions is significantly more costly at $499. Together with the machine include the accessories such as Cricut cartridges that are likewise not easy in the pocket. It's possible to acquire affordable Cricut Cartridges and machines at the world wide web in addition to from additional specialty shop. You only need to know where to search.

By placing a little effort in comparing costs, it's no problem to locate bargains in your Cricut printer machines in addition to cartridges and other accessories. There are lots of craft shops which you are able to visit throughout their voucher specials. JoAnn Fabrics, Michaels and Hobby Lobby are a few of the very popular craft shops which sell Cricut accessories and machines. Look out for your weekly earnings from other community craft shops.

Paper Crafting Pro provides some excellent bargains up to 20 and less. You can't get their pricing in case you don't enroll online. The enrollment, however, isn't totally free. You have to pay $9.99 for your monthly fee. If you're in a company of disposing cartridges, to enroll is a fantastic thing, however, as you've got monthly charges to cover, start looking for different sites which don't charge membership fees.

You may also purchase more affordable Cricut cartridges out of eBay. You're able to score on a brand newchance under $15 buck. Even though you've got to run on the capsules, you simply need to be patient and be inclined to bidding . As a result, you can prevent overpaying for the capsule. Lookout for transport fees. Find vendors who provide free shipment inside the US land. You might even bidding Cricut Cake capsules which generally cost around $100 that you are able to acquire on the internet for $25 or not. Many do not realize that but Cricut Cake capsules may be utilised in almost any Cricut machine.

Oh my scrapbooking is really a site which consistently sells Cricut cartridges in a reduce cost. Their cartridges can charge

$30 and under. You are able to register to their email newsletter and receive coupons for up to 20% off.

There you've got it. It is not really tough to search for affordable Cricut cartridges once you know the best place to look. Always remember: not cover the complete cost of a Cricut chance or for dispatch that prices you over $30.

Device Is ripping or pulling through my stuff

There are several factors that might give rise to a system to rip through substance. Luckily, this issue can normally be solved with a few simple troubleshooting measures. In case a Cricut Maker or Cricut Explore device is ripping or dragging throughout the content, assess the following:

- make certain you have chosen the suitable content placing in Design Space or the Smart Position Dial is about the right setting.

- If you're using the customized setting, make certain that the suitable material is chosen from the drop-down listing.

- Confirm the size and intricacy of this picture. If you're cutting a picture that's quite complicated or little, consider cutting out a simpler or bigger.

- When trimming on a easy picture resolves the matter, consider cutting the intricate image utilizing the customized setting for Cardstock - Intricate Cuts.

- If employing a Cricut Explore Air two or Cricut Maker in Quick Mode, turn Quick Mode away and try your trimming again.

- Eliminate the blade home in the device, then get rid of the blade and also look for any debris within the home or onto the blade.

- Reduce pressure configurations for that substance type from the Manage Custom Materials display by means of 2-4. Get the Manage Custom Materials display through the accounts menu or by choosing Edit Custom Materials at the top from your Mat Preview display once you click on Change Material.

- That might have to be performed 2-3 days to alter the trimming result.

- Try cutting another substance -- like copy paper at the proper setting for this material. It might be an issue with this particular substance which you're working to cut.

- Try with a fresh mat and blade. Both can lead to cut problems.

- When the problem persists after you've completed each these measures, please contact Member Care through a few of the choices below for more help.

CHAPTER SEVEN
THINGS TO KNOW ABOUT CRICUT

Cricut Comparisons - Which to Buy?

There are currently 5 Cricut machine versions. They're made by the Provo Craft business. How can you know which to purchase? In the event you begin small or move large off the bat? I will offer you the details of every one in easy terms so you can create your own choice on what is right for you. We will discuss the 4 primary machines. There's currently a Cricut Cake system, but it's so much like this Cricut Expression, I am not likely to pay that you especially.

Let us Split down it

Original Cricut: (aka Baby Bug)

- Mat dimensions = 6 x 12

- Could utilize all cartridges

- Can utilize all of blades and housings

- Can utilize markers

- Cuts any size newspaper that suits about the mat

Makes cuts that range from 1 inch to 5-1/2 inches in

dimension, in half inch increments.

Could connect to a PC and use Design Studio or Certainly Cuts lots Computer Software

Cricut Produce: (Type of a hybrid of this Baby Bug and also the saying. It's still modest, but includes a number of the qualities of this Cricut Expression)

- May utilize all cartridges

- May utilize all of blade and housings

- May utilize markers

- Cuts any size newspaper that suits around the mat

- Makes cuts that range from 1/4 inch into 11-1/2 inches in dimension, in quarter inch increments.

- Can link to a PC and use Design Studio or Positive Cuts lots Computer Software

- Has any innovative attribute buttons (reverse, fit to page, match to span, centre stage, etc..)

- Can link to a PC and use Design Studio or Positive Cuts lots Computer Software

Cricut Length:

- Mat dimensions = 12 x 12, or 12 x 24

- Could utilize all cartridges

- Can utilize all of blades and housings

- Could utilize markers

- Cuts any size newspaper that is suitable for on size pad

Makes cuts out of 1/4 inch into 23-1/2 inches in dimension, in quarter inch increments.

Has lots of innovative attribute buttons (reverse, fit to page, match to span, centre stage, etc..)

Has style keys (amount, auto load, portrait, etc..)

Could link to a PC and work with Design Studio or Certain Cuts lots Computer Software

Cricut Picture: (Newest & greatest version. The design of this Cricut machine using a colour printer)

- Mat dimensions = 12 x 12 (unique Dark mat)

- May utilize all cartridges

- Can utilize all of blades and housings

- Cuts or eyeglasses or equally on any size document that suits on mat

- Makes cuts out of 1/4 inch into 11-1/2 inches in dimension, in quarter inch increments

- Has lots of imaginative attributes (turn, fit on page, match to span, centre point, etc..)

- Has manners (amount, auto match, portrait, etc..)

- The device will print the picture and then cut it.

Comes with an LCD display and runs on the stylus for browsing the display

Same Accessories are compatible with machines. The cartridgesblades, tools and markers aren't machine-specific. The cutting pads are the sole thing that change based upon the machine. The new Picture also needs the new mat. The aged green mats won't work with this.

If You're wanting this system for portability, size and weight may be a variable for you.

Weight Dimensions

Private Cricut 7 Lbs. 15.5" x 7" x 7"

Cricut Produce 10.75 Lbs 15.5" x 7" x 7"

Cricut Expression 13.4 Lbs. 21.5" x 7" x 7.75"

Cricut Picture 28 Lbs. 23.5" x 9" x13.5"

Personal and produce are equally small, mobile lightweight machines. If you're taking your endeavors to plants or distinct tasks then you may wish to think about one of these. They're lightweight and easy to go around. The Expression is a lot heavier and bigger. In case you've got a craft area or room to scrapbooking so you don't have to transfer it frequently, you get a lot more choices with this system.

Cricut Accessories For Scrapbooking

When in regards to a scrapbooking, the ideal accessories will make all of the difference. That is the reason it is a fantastic concept to select Circuit accessories to the scrapbook needs so you know that you're receiving quality scrapbooking items that you may depend on.

When you would like assistance with your scrapbooking, then Cricut is a title you can rely on to supply you with quality tools and accessories that will assist you make good scrapbooking. By way of instance, you may take your topics and thoughts and make them a reality in ways you wouldn't have been able to do before.

With that the Cricut cuts along with other accessories, so you could be as imaginative as you desire. If you do not believe you are a really artistic or creative individual, you may make use of these tools to produce things that you never would have been in a position to consider earlier. If you're creative, then you are able to take that imagination even further using all the resources which Cricut can provide for you.

You can make use of these resources to your benefit to make a number of the greatest scrapbooks about. Your thoughts can become a fact so it's going to be easier than ever before to capture those pictures and mementos coordinated into scrapbooks that you cherish forever.

When deciding upon those accessories, create a record of

the ones that you want and want the most. Then return in order beginning with the ones which you want the maximum and moving down into the ones that you'd like to have since you are able to afford it. Then you're able to buy these one or 2 at a time before your group is complete and you've got each the excellent Cricut accessories that you need on your scrapbook sets.

Here are merely a couple of those safest accessories out there:

- Deep Cut Blades

- Cricut Stamp Refill

- Cricut Jukebox

- Cricut Cartridge Storage Box

- Cricut Color Fashion

- Cricut Cutting Mats

- Cricut Spatula Tool

Now That you learn more about picking Cricut accessories such as scrapbooking, then you are able to apply this on your personal scrapbooking. You may discover that it makes your scrapbooking much simpler and it also provides you more layouts and more ways to utilize your imagination for exceptional scrapbooking.

Cricut Expression - Worth the Money

The Cricut Expression is selling like hot cakes on the web! What is all of the fuss about? Here I shall provide you a fast collection of the very best characteristics, and enable you to determine if the Cricut filler actually cuts !

- The Cricut Expression is a really sophisticated crafting device, compared to Cricut Create along with also the Cricut Personal Electronic Cutter. The very first thing strikes you is just how large this new version is, with regard to its dimensions.

- It's been fabricated by a group of seasoned specialists with the only purpose cutting letters, letters, and contours in appropriate sizes throughout the use of this 12 inches x 24 inches cutting mat.

- This superb electronic model may perform different kinds of paper clippings such as vellum and maybe even vinyl. Crafters can cut paper to little .25 inch bits, and around 12 inches x 24 inches.

- Different layouts with a vast assortment of contours can be drawn up via this complex device.

- It's packed with unique attributes like Plantin faculty publication font and Accent Critical type capsules, inclusive of this 12 x 12 mat for cutting functions.

- Cricut certainly made Expression with teachers and schools in your mind. This system could be popular set up in the course space, there is little doubt about this!

- The most recent model generates an impressively high number of distinct paper cuts. But, crafters considering forming dices measuring less than 51/2 inches may nevertheless elect for your Cricut.

- The most important drawback could be that many crafters discover that it's tricky to produce sufficient space for the setup of the outer machine, because of the bulky casing.

- In addition to the core attributes, you get welcome bonuses such as, Vehicle Load, Mix'n Match, Fit to Page, Flip and Fit to Style etc.. This updated model can be packed with all the Accent Cartridge that will surely develop the attribute of scrapbook designs.

- Together with the awesome Flip choice, you are able to track the image or chart changing its instructions. This is much more entertaining than it seems!

- The center point process is a real-time saver. It helps users to place the blade over the authentic center indicating of this photograph or picture, then trims the particular place on the photograph for you - really convenient.

- The multi-cut mechanism allows the unit to reduce thick sized chipboard considerably deeper than previously.

- The Line spin placing helps you to fix the blade into another line when performing heavy cuts.

- Additionally the Mat Size program will permit the user to place 12 inches x 24 inches or 12 inches x 12 inches.

Cricut Design Studio Help For Newbies - 5 minutes Tutorial!

Switch on your PC! If you have successfully set up on your Cricut Design Studio applications you need to observe the tiny green Cricut Bug appearing at you with large eyes directly out of your desktop computer.

When you load the program, you are going to be shown a huge window with elements that may appear odd (or not so odd) at first glance.

Here is a brief description of the chief things in the Cricut Design Studio applications to assist the newcomer (you!) Begin without yanking your hair to hair loss because the program's manual is a bit too lean:

1. the very first thing you'll see is that the digital mat that appears just like your bodily pad. That is your digital design area and where the majority of the action will occur. Begin by clicking on some other form in the keypad overlay (the major box only in addition to the mat) and play with the picture. You will see huge circles round the contour, these are known as"selection manages" plus they allow you to control and distort the picture in each direction.

2. The next thing you'll see is, as discussed in the past stage, the keypad overlay. This is the digital keypad which changes in line with the cartridges you have chosen. Each single time you click one the letters or shapes on it will show up on your digital mat so that you play it and layout exactly what you would like.

3. Third would be the two boxes only contrary to the keypad overlay: the chance library around the left and also the form properties box to your right.The chance library is precisely what its name implies, it is sort of an indicator of all of the cartridges out there. You are able to design to any of those cartridges and also utilize letters or shapes from various cartridges at precisely the exact same design but you will have the ability to cut just with all the cartridges you have (not trendy! ... I understand). The contour properties box allows you control the

selected letters or shapes with more accuracy. You're able to provide them X and Y coordinates (like back in college), you may give them exact height and width, it is possible to rotate themyou can nudge themweld them kern them.

What is nudging? Clicking the nudging switches moves the form you pick by very tiny increments. Use it if you have to make tiny alterations.

What is Welding? Welding allows you to have contours"glued" together if you cut them together with all the cricut. Simply make letters or shapes overlap in your style, when you flip the weld operate onto these overlapping letters will probably be glued together once you reduce them.

What is kerning? Kerning let's you define the distance between phrases. Utilize it to have a predetermined number (positive or negative) between phrases without needing to nudge them over and over again.

Matters To recall:

You can Layout along with all the cartridges which exist in the world (do not know for Other planets) however you can just cut together with all the ones that you've bought.

You May Use Other folks cut documents in case your not in a really creative mood. Just head Into the cricut message board or perform a fast search on Google to get "cricut layout studio trimming documents".

Make sure to upgrade your software if needed to become new cartridges packed in your cartridge library and to find bug fixes.

CONCLUSION

When in regards to arts and crafts, so you may never fail with Cricut Cartridges. In order to get many of years, lots of aspiring artists are inspired by different layouts and patterns offered by the capsules created by Cricut. Regular, a great deal of shops can market a small number of capsules because of growing demand of those products as soon as it comes to neighborhood shops. With the popularity of this line, a great deal of retailers also has been effective in leasing to your brand. For people that aren't into arts and crafts, then you might not understand a whole lot about Cricut capsules. But, we guarantee you that understanding more about those products can help yourself participate in more activities concerning paper crafts.

The finest thing concerning Cricut cartridges is that you don't ever appear to run out of ideas and choices. Whether you adore fonts, shapes or animation characters, you'll have the ability to locate a cartridge which can fit your taste. But when choosing a cartridge out of Cricut, the very first thing which you will need to take into account is how far your budget will probably be. The selection of costs of these capsules can appear as low as just a bit below fifty dollars, and may soar alongside a hundred bucks.

If you're the sort of person who enjoys a great deal of colors, you are able to stick with the fundamental silhouette cartridges and just take advantage of different colored papers to perform your cutouts. If you would rather create use of words, then state for the scrapbook designs, you might even use the ribbon cartridges. Additionally, there are people who are a massive fan of this certified character collection. You'll have the ability to use cutouts of your favorite cartoon characters from Disney and other animated movies. For many adults who have kids in your home, this is going to be a superb chance to bond with your kids and educate them how to generate their own art bits.

CRICUT DESIGN SPACE

The Ultimate Step-by-Step Guide for Beginners to Start and Mastering Cricut Design Space and Learn Tips and Tricks Create your Perfect Ideas.

Rachel Baker

DISCLAIMER

All erudition contained in this book is given for informational and educational purposes only. The author is not in any way accountable for any results or outcomes that emanate from using this material. Constructive attempts have been made to provide information that is both accurate and effective, but the author is not bound for the accuracy or use/misuse of this information.

FOREWORD

irst, I will like to thank you for taking the first step of trusting me and deciding to purchase/read this life-transforming eBook. Thanks for spending your time and resources on this material.

I can assure you of exact results if you will diligently follow the exact blueprint, I lay bare in the information manual you are currently reading. It has transformed lives, and I strongly believe it will equally transform your own life too.

All the information I presented in this Do It Yourself piece is easy to digest and practice.

INTRODUCTION

C rafting is one of the very famous hobbies in the world nowadays. It is possible to discover lots of men, women and even children who enjoy crafting plus some who make a professional living out of it. You will find a lot of unique tools, supplies and software programs available to help these crafting lovers make the most of the instant.

The cricut machine is only that. It is an electronic cutter that helps with paper crafts. With just a bit of a button you can produce beautiful designs and get help with crafts for home decor, scrapbooking, paper crafting and a whole lot more. The machine is rather straightforward to navigate and use so the 1 thing which you truly must be worried about is being creative and enabling your creativity run rampant.

There is no need for a computer to use the cricut apparatus. All you'll need is a normal electrical outlet to plug it right into and you are ready to go. Before you start it is beneficial to bring a small bit of time and make more comfortable with this machine. Take a peek at the the paper feed to understand how everything works.

The on button, clip button and stop button is going to be grouped with the right of the device, the paper feed at the back.

To get began, first ascertain what crafts you would like to work on. Place a cricut cartridge into the device and you get to pick from several designs, sizes and get every detail in the manner. There are thousands of possibilities so the designs you are able to produce with your crafting are infinite.

There is a user guide that contains the machine as soon as you purchase it give this a read in the event you're experiencing some difficulties. The cricut system is a priceless investment for any crafter who selects their own hobby seriously.

With cricut cutting machines for your craft projects

More and more people are choosing to produce their own scrapbooking materials, invitations and holiday cards. These do-it-yourself options allow a good deal more space for customization in contrast to their mass generated options. Not only are home made invitations considerably more customizable, but they also cost considerably less than store - bought choices. Circut personal cutting machines also make it possible for people who have minimal time and even less experience to make professional looking craft projects anytime.

Cricut cutting machines are available locally in craft stores along with a department stores that contain craft and artwork sections. On the flip side, the very best deals are often located online. For the occasional do-it-your self, the entry level version, together with readily available sale prices of roughly $100 is more than sufficient. It is more than capable of creating a massive number of different shape combinations and requires hardly any upkeep. More experienced crafters, or individuals who manage home businesses that produce customized paper products, may find that larger models are more compared with their requirements.

All those machines are semi automatic, and a lot simpler to use than manual paper cutters. Generally, they can cut very heavy paper stock, allowing scrapbookers to produce layouts with several distinct colors and textures. For information on the best way to utilize a system, there are a selection of sites offering advice from regular amateur clients. They are a significant source of the inspiration and data, showing the method by which in which the machine could be best used. Whenever these sites are a great destination for those that are only starting, the very best characteristic of a home cricut machine is the capability to make fully one-of-a-kind web pages. Experiment with new form and colour combinations to earn something memorable and distinctive.

Cricut cutting machines are adaptable enough to be used for any kind of craft occupation.

Make professional searching scrapbooks with circut personal cutting machines

A circut cutting machine is vital have for any scrapbooker.

These machines make it possible for customers to cut paper into some selection of fascinating shapes, making personalizing each page in a scrapbook easy and pleasurable. Made to be little enough to bring with you when you journey, they will occupy little space in your home and could be carried with you for just about any scrapbooking parties you could attend. They are the perfect tool for everyone who is looking for a user friendly means of producing specific bounds, sew or other page vases.

Cricut machines can create shapes that are anywhere from 1" to over 5" tall. Straightforward to change metal cutting patterns are used to create uniform shapes in many sorts of craft paper. These forms could be utilized to add custom decoration, festive shapes or interesting boundaries which could reflect the material of each page. As many distinctive thicknesses of card stock may be used, scrapbookers have to be aware that newspaper in a milder tier may cause the blades to dull quicker. This typically means that you need to always keep a tab on the sharpness of the blade and then replace them if necessary to maintain superior outcomes.

A cricut machine is not a small investment. Prices start at approximately $100 online, which could place this cutting edge device out of reach for a few. But when taking under account the purchase price of purchasing packs of pre-cut letters and shapes, most committed scrapbook enthusiasts do locate the machine will eventually pay for itself. It might also be used for extra paper based crafts, such as making custom invitations, gift tags and holiday cards. The cricut company has a fantastic standing in the crafting world, and their products are definitely going to be lasting, hence no replacement should be demanded, even with heavy use.

Scrapbooking is becoming more popular than ever especially with the guidance of all cricut cartridges. Developing a scrapbook may be fun for the entire family. It is a creative way to preserve family history with photographs, journal entries, and memorabilia. Implementing a cricut expression cutting machine together with its tremendous library of cricut capsules makes pictures previously come home to your future generations!

Shortly adhering to the production of photographs, people started creating ideas of how to maintain the photos for safekeeping. In the 15th centuryas cheap paper became available to the average citizen in England, scrapbooks called insignificant books were kept to put away quotes, poetry, correspondence, and recipes.

Subsequently as now, every scrapbook was unique to the author's specific theme. In the 16th century, friendship files were the rage. These documents were similar to modern day yearbooks, where friends sign each others yearbook in the end of the school year.

All these creative outlets afforded women in subsequent

generations with opportunities to develop their literary skills by documenting their history. It might be hard for us to imagine now but girls living before the 18th and 19th centuries generally did not have the capability to read and write made readily available for them.

The producers of provo craft certainly do not want to come across these days return where women were saved in the dark! In fact, they churn out creations all year long with every passing year to help bring our imagination and imagination to light. For instance, the handy cricut jukebox was made for scrapbookers to conveniently preserve the majority of the cricut capsules effortlessly. Implementing the jukeboxes, there is no need to stop your creative flow if you'd like to modify out cartridges.

Apart from the newly published old west and hannah montana, you'll discover wonderful classics such as disney mickey font cartridge and christmas solutions cartridge. Two of my personal favorites, which I have been amazed at the tasks results, are the home accents solutions cartridge and the home decor solutions cartridge. If you've ever wondered precisely what provo craft suggests by infinite chances in their slogan take a peek at those impressive capsules!

Use your cricut machine to generate money scrapbooking

If you're into scrapbooking at all then no doubt you have heard about provo craft's cricut cutting machines. They are amazing machines that take a fantastic deal of work from a lot of jobs, they don't require a computer to use, plus they are so simple and intuitive to comprehend much we can understand them! In case you've ever used one then you almost certainly have noticed exactly how much pleasure they are, but have you ever thought about how to make money doing what you love?

Making money from this flame is a dream of many, but they usually believe that it's too hard and give up. The simple fact remains that doing this isn't really that hard! The only limit is your imagination and what it's possible to make. Here's a couple of tips to get you started using wondering how the method to make some money with your hobby:

Decorate themed parties

Kids love to own themed parties. Whether it is a pokemon party, a bakugan birthday party, a disney character costume celebration, kids simply love them. You can easily earn some money by producing decoration packs for these kinds of events. Print and cut out a great deal of different sized decorations, produce customized name tags that the kids can adhere, create playing cards or perhaps character cards which the kids can accumulate and exchange together.

Custom cards and invitations

Who doesn't love a personalized thank you card or invitation? It shows a fantastic deal of thought and love has gone into them. If you enjoy doing this, why not sell any of your creations to make a little money at exactly the specific same instant? It is really surprising how a great deal of people would really like to receive a custom made card or invite made for the birthdays, anniversaries, get-togethers, and particular events. Fairly frequently you local arts and crafts store are even inclined to put your creations on screen and market them to get their clientele. Evidently, they often have a cut, but in addition, it saves you the time of having to go out and find people yourself.

Custom scrapbook layouts

Scrapbooking can border to a obsession with us. We're continuously attempting to make this perfect page layout, or find the ideal touch that may make our scrapbooks that better. It is possible to use the cricut method to make die cuts of record page layouts and sell them to other fans on your own. When it's your fire then it will be no difficulty thinking up a couple of to-die-for layouts!

Produce a website

You can consistently promote your items on the internet. Nowadays it is quite simple to create a web site. Proceed to blogger.com and register to find a totally free website, then with only a little practice you will have the ability to generate a superb little website featuring all the terrific products that you provide. Put it on a business card (also free with lots of those online offers in the marketplace) and pass it out to anyone that you meet. They can easily be able to observe all you supply in 1 place and place an order.

All these are just a couple ideas which you start making money with your hobbies. Don't be intimidated and think you are not good enough or it is too hard. Just start striving, and you could wind up amazed at how good your efforts turn out.

Cricut scrapbook number one thought

The number 1 best idea to utilize your cricut on is to make something on your own little ones!

Kids love to follow all kinds of stories. However 1 story they probably would want to hear over and over again is that the narrative of the birth. That's why, many might prefer making baby scrapbook to notify in a more tangible manner how they appear on earth. But, it does not signify that infant scrapbook is limited to the"how" of giving birth. Even the tiny details are crucial to make a much more amazing baby scrapbook your kid would enjoy and are proud of as they grow. And since infant scrapbook is a tiny kid's bibliography, your kids will love exactly how much they mean to you.

If you plan to utilize your cricut device to make a scrapbook for your baby in advance, then below are a few things which you have to think about so that you wont confine yourself from creating a baby scrapbook (infant scrapbook that only tells the time, dimensions and weight of your baby).

To make a child scrapbook, you will need to define your starting point. It might be the baby shower or even the day of their birth. In addition, you will need to set when to complete the scrapbook. Usually, baby scrapbook will assure the child's first year nonetheless, you can always go longer if you'd love to. In the process, you want to collect things that might be included on the scrapbook like the gifts you receive on the baby shower. Some may even incorporate the baby's first haircut together with different events that the child has gotten for the very first moment.

Elect to get a colour that will define the subject of the scrapbook. The normal color of a baby boy's scrapbook is powder blue while the baby girl's record is pink. You might or may not adapt these colors and use another.

Now you request:"imagine should I comprise from the scrapbook?"

Most baby scrapbook could incorporate the truth about the baby upon birth. These are, the time of birth, weight at birth, time of birth, the length of work, the color of the eyes and hair, and doctor's name and the names of the group who assisted the doctor in providing birth. And needless to say, the pictures of you and your child in the hospital after you gave birth.

Some would include pictures of you since you are still pregnant. Moments such as this will help keep your child reminded how you, as a mother cared for him was on your uterus.

Added seconds you want to add are the photos of the baby's development month by month working with a measurement reference (generally a stuffed toy), photos of the house you live in and also the nursery, photos of the family members like the baby, photos of the baby sleeping, photos taken while the baby is bathing, photos together with their favourite toys, and other joyous moments that comprise them.

As was mentioned before, many baby scrapbooks could include the baby's firsts. These are the baby's first smile, first toilet first crawl, first roster over, first sat up steps, etc.. Baby scrapbook might include their favourites like the favourite song, toys, bedtime stories, along with the shrub.

The nice thing about this is that you can always add whatever's connected to your kid as he or she is growing up.

For additional vital events that may or may not be captured by memorabilia could be written.

You can write about the significance and worth of the name, your time of stay at the hospital, further women and men that were present at the hospital, their answer after you gave birth, their own feelings whenever they carried your baby, and how they entertain the baby. Perhaps you will write about stories that could further exemplify these events that are listed in photos. Stories like the baby's first flashes, babysitting, and mannerisms (did he or she often suck their thumb... And matters like people).

CHAPTER ONE
ADVANCED CRICUT
TECHNIQUES

Cricut is a renowned manufacturer of equipment drifting everywhere in the country. It is an exciting and one of a type gadget used by numerous men and women who would like to produce creative and superior jobs. As of this moment, there are just three different versions of cricut: the cricut generate machine, high-end cricut expression and naturally, the base version cricut personal electronic cutter machine.

Before improving concerning what cricut can foster the society, let's take a look during its history. Cricut was initially made with a massive company named provo craft which was a tiny store. About forty decades ago, the company of provo craft started as a retail store in the small town of provo, utah. With their resourcefulness and creativity, the company eventually enlarged after the amount of decades. They finally have a total of ten stores with up to 200,000 foot distribution center.

If you examine the normal cricut machine, it appears like the expression of a inkjet printer. But it doesn't require a pc to be worked at all. A mean person can use its function since you do not need programming abilities too. One of its advantages include being lightweight. Its blade might even cut thin and thick newspapers ranging between 1 inch and 5.5 inches in height.

Cricut just weighs half lbs and that has the power adapter. What is more, it's likely to bring it anyplace such as party parties or event demonstrations because it's a portable product. Using its distinctive and sleek design, it will always appear suitable for almost any crafting office.

As mentioned before, it may cut to 5.5 inches but that's just 1 feature it contains. It may cut borders and names around eleven inches , hence, making it an ideal fit to a paper by means of a dimension of 12x12 inches. Unlike other producers, cricut's most important facet is having the capability to cut a great deal of stuff. Cricut can also cut on a paper which has a broad variety of around 0.5 mm thick. Luckily, provo craft has supplied additional materials such as designer paper pads and cardstock pads which could be used jointly with cricut cartridges. In reality, these two different sorts of papers are made to have a perfect match with cricut.

Even in the event you ask many customers of cricut, they'd definitely state that cricut electronic cutter is the best one of the very best cutters. This is only because cricut cartridges have a massive group of choices with respect to styles, fonts and designs, therefore, boosting the most degree of imagination without the necessity of a pc.

If you don't know using cricut cartridges, they are mini inserts that you set inside the cricut for you to set the kind of shape, layout, font or layout that you would like to cut. The cartridge even has distinct classes. It includes: ribbon cartridges, licensed capsules, form capsules, choices capsules and classmate cartridges.

Finally, you are very lucky since buying a cricut cutter also entitles one to receive one free cartridge! This free cartridge includes some basic contours that might already offer you the opportunity to make a number of shapes and decoration. If not happy, you can purchase additional cricut capsules to add up to your collection. The more capsules you have, the higher odds of creating unique artworks.

5 Steps To Creating Beautiful Designs With The Cricut Personal Electronic Cutter

The cricut personal electronic cutter must by now be familiar to anybody at all interested in home crafts, and specifically scrapbooking. If you are a newcomer to this world, then suffice it to say the cricut personal electronic cutter is a radical cutting tool that can effortlessly cut any design or shape you'll be able to think about. From the time you've read this manual, you should become a fantastic deal more clued up on exactly what this system (or more exactly, this assortment of machines) has to give you.

The aim of this manual is to supply a simple five step

process you'll be able to use so as to use a cricut personal electronic cutter to create a visually magnificent layout. I'll flesh out each of the measures along with the notion procedures you will experience, and the choices you'll have to make. After all, you'll have the ability to go off and create actual something that is currently stuck in your own imagination.

Have a thought

The first measure to making your masterpiece is a notion. However complicated the technology you are using, it's useless if you do not possess some inspiration to begin with. It can be that you know exactly what it is you're attempting to achieve - state a scrapbook page for your child's school sports day or even a family reunion. You might not be quite as sure - in which case I advocate a fast search on google for"scrapbooking site" or comparable. Take a browse through a few of these websites which return, and you're going to discover almost endless inspiration very fast.

Which cricut?

If you don't already have a cricut personal electronic cutter - you'll have to decide at this point which one matches your requirements. You decision will likely be based upon your budget, and if you will need anything more than basic cutting-edge functions. The exact details about what each variant can do and how far they buy is beyond the scope of this manual, but this information is publicly available on the internet.

Select a cartridge

The next measure is to decide on a proper cartridge at the cricut choice. Again, going into detail about the cricut capsule process is outside of scope for this particular article - the very best option would be to go and browse through the many available cartridges online at amazon or comparable. It is possible to get cartridges with layouts and shapes for almost anything you may think about all cartridges are compatible with every cricut personal electronic cutter version.

Customize your cut

With an thought, a machine alongside a capsule in place, you are nearly there. The previous decision making point is to select how you wish to personalize your layout along with the additional choices onboard to cricut personal electronic cutter. This option includes the measurements of the program, and functions like page, stretch-to-fit and tons of others.

Hit a button

Finally, all your project is finished - you simply have to load on your card or paper and hit the start button.

If you abide by these five easy steps, you can go out of a spark of inspiration into an expert jaw-dropping design in super fast time. I hope you've got fun in the process, and get the results you're searching for!

Tips which might help you to begin

Capturing memories on a digital camera, an HD camera, and a voice recorder make life more meaningful. Whenever there's a special moment that you would like to catch and be in a position to return to at any particular time, you can do this easily with the guidance of those tools. Nonetheless, pictures are still the favourite medium by the majority of people. When you would like to put together those images and compile them on a distinctive souvenir, then you turn to scrapbooking.

Scrapbooking is a method of preservation of memories which has been around for quite a while and it's evolved so much better. In earlier times the creation of a single scrapbook was a monumentally mad job. Now, however, with the creation of devices like the cricut cutting machine, items are made easier. If you're seeking to making a scrapbook, this poor boy is the tool for you. There are numerous great cricut ideas on the market which you might make the most of.

Scrapbooks are just a few of the many cricut thoughts on the market. This tool, if you understand how to optimize it can help you in creating items which go beyond scrapbooking for example calendars. Should you purchase a cricut cartridge, then you will find a ton of designs uploaded in each one. These pre- made themes might be used for a great deal of items such as hangings such as walls, picture frames, picture frames, picture frames, picture frames, and greeting cards for several seasons.

Just your creativity will restrict your progress with a cricut machine. Together with calendars, you are able to design every month to reflect the weather, the disposition, and particular events that are linked with that. The cricut machine may look after that. But in case one cartridge does not have the design that search, you can always go and buy. It's that simple!

Cricut machines might be somewhat expensive with the price beginning at $299. That is pretty hefty for anybody to start with. Be a smart buyer. You may always turn into the net web to look for great deals on cricut machines. Purchasing from ebay may also be a great move but can take numerous risks if you are not experienced with ebay. If you're very worried about this, you can always await a sale to happen at one of those regional malls and purchase out there since it will likely have a warranty.

Those are just one of the many great cricut thoughts available on the marketplace. Calendars along with a great deal of could be made with the use of this marvelous machine. Remember, just your imagination can limit what you could do.

The Top Ten Reasons Why I Chose to Purchase Cricut Personal Cutter

Why are you into paper crafting? Do you do a lot of scrapbooking? I've been into those for a little while today, and I have to say, among the most troublesome elements is to cut on my letters or shapes. It just takes forever. Recently I had been introduced into the cricut personal cutter that is an automated cutting system that does all this boring project for you. So I did a little research on this particular product, and was finally convinced I wish to purchase it. Within this column I will reveal the best 5 reason why I opted to buy cricut personal cutter.

*enjoy the simplicity of cutting an assortment of sizes

In comparison to additional cutting edge systems, using cricut personal cutter, you can fix the system to reduce any measurements of shapes or letters between 1 to 5.5 inches. Previously, in order for me to cut particular contours with a normal die cut system I needed to have different templates for every letter and each size of those letters. The excellent thing about my option to purchase cricut personal cutter is I didn't want all these different templates.

*it is light and easy to carry

Cricut private cutter is really simple to carry around, contrary to other large and hefty die cut machines.

Additionally, you might also buy a carrying tote for it. It is simple to take it to some friends' house and also have a scrapbooking party together. And in case you ever need to move on your cricut personal cutter, then it will not be a problem at all.

*it is compact and conserves space

When you purchase cricut personal cutter, you don't need to prepare a great deal of room to keep it. It is quite compact and does not occupy a substantial volume of distance. Additionally, you don't need to go through the problem of maintaining dividers of templates, for example with older fashioned die cut machines. It's not hard to put your cricut personal cutter in your desk without it taking up way too much distance.

*it functions good for any sorts of endeavors

Whether you are in the mood to get some scrapbooking, or developing a birthday card for a friend, or maybe helping your kid with a college project, you can pretty much use your cricut personal cutter for anything you desire. It's various shapes and features you might utilize. I have to acknowledge, when working with the cricut personal cutter, the moment you get those creative juices flowing, then there are no limits in what it's possible to make.

*it is automatic and higher tech.

Rather of needing to manually cut each letter or form one,

together with the cricut personal cutter, everything is automatic. All you need to do is set your paper on the mat, then follow a few directions, and press a few buttons, and the cutter can do all of the hard work for you. This is a great feature as you may set your own cricut own cutter to begin cutting some thing, as you are able to do anything else in the exact same moment. This makes scrapbooking a breeze.

As it's possible for you to see from these top five reasons why I chose to buy cricut personal cutter, this is a really valuable tool which can enable you not cut several different dimensions, but in addition create any endeavor you need, with its high tech port. Therefore don't be scared to have a look at this wonderful instrument, and see how the cricut personal cutter will help save you money and time on your paper craft projects because it's helped me.

Being a crafty individual has never been simpler using the cricut measure two. This handy-dandy thing of equipment has made it simple and fun to create your private craft jobs unique and personal to your vision. Being like the cricut expression 2 isn't the first of its type (hence both) the new slick design along with the entire colour lcd touch screen display with stylus shows its expansion with the times. Let us be honest, we don't like things to work well we also all secretly want it to look good also.

Scrap booking can be of a creative outlet than a hobby together with the many features the cricut expression 2 must provide you with. But don't make the mistake of believing that you are only restricted to scrap booking since it is possible to use this to any creative project you are doing or perhaps add to ones which you've already done. Together with the cricut the possibilities are infinite!

Contrary to newest buys you make this instrument includes two wealthy capsules being the alphabet cartridge and yet another being the essentials cartridge. The alphabet cartridge is exactly what you'll use for numbers, letters and designs giving life to whatever you write. No more plain jane letters and numbers since utilizing the cricut expression two plain isn't ever a choice.

Now let us talk about the vital cartridge. "why?" you may ask? Well let me tell you this multi-purpose cartridge is where the creative pleasure begins! With this cartridge you are going to be able to get a lot of designs, shapes and art that can open your mind and get those creative juices flowing so that projects can become the masterpieces you intended them to be. Attributes like mat trailer to let you see till you commit. Additionally, there are material settings so you may have your project to perfection consequently. Moreover, you'll have a cutting position light to help with the exact cuts you need done. There's definitely somebody in the cricut development office that's attempting to please the customer!

It constantly means more when you or someone you love makes some thing from scratch to you since they must put a great deal of energy and thought behind it to actually sit down and make it. The cricut expression 2 permits every person to open up a brand-new technique of production. In the event you've never have tapped into your internal craftiness it is possible to use the expression two to enlarge your own ideas to what choices there are. Along with the beauty in this is your liberty you've got while having the choice to express yourself without the guidance of hallmark or any other important fabrication.

Imagine how refreshing it is to allow yourself know who you are and having the ability to prove that self within an artistic fashion employing the cricut measure 2. Sometimes we get so wrapped up in our daily lives we don't take the opportunity to measure in the daily routine and also do something that we can genuinely appreciate. So quit restricting yourself and start expressing yourself have some fun!

CHAPTER TWO
THE CRICUT EXPRESSION

I f you wish to make matters work out to you in just about any endeavour that you pick, you would like more than just the energy and determination. To make the long story short, you will need tools or tools. The same as an aspiring guitar player, you can't develop in the best if you don't have a guitar. The cost of a guitar isn't a laughing matter but however expensive it is, you want to have it in case you'd like to advance. However, if you're wise, you can discover your tool at a lower price.

The same concept applies to some aspiring scrapbook manufacturer. Even though it's a simple fact that the cricut machine is in factnot the cheapest, you can't deny that this is a required tool. But, despite being a requirement for making decorations, it carries with it a hefty price. The normal cost for a single cricut machine starts at $299. Now it is expensive for an entire lot. Are there some ways you may find something more affordable? Yes, there actually is. If you know where to look, you'll make certain to find one that is less in your wallet and bang for quality. This is where you flip into a cricut sale.

Google could be very a powerful tool in times like this. In the event you enter any important word when it comes to economical cricut term machines, then then the search engine will supply you with a substantial assortment of search outcomes. The first results that you find on the very first few pages are always the best ones that you need to see .

Another alternative is to find online from sites such as eBay or amazon. Only be tired of these people which you do business. General rule is to always conduct background checks into the people who you decide to transact with. You may accomplish that by clicking on their profile and seeing exactly how much good feedback was allowed to them. If they're given a fantastic deal of starts, he or she is credible.

From the occasion that you are still fairly far against buying online and you insist on purchasing from a local store, you can do most certainly do that. An excellent way to locate cheap cricut expression machines would be by means of mall earnings. The principle here is to turn into a careful and wise buyer. Never buy when something is not offered.

Cricut cartridge review for life is a beach

What can you think about when you hear the expression summer? I think of the sea and shore. And life is a beach cricut capsule is all about summer and getting pleasure for me .

With this capsule it is likely to go out of using lemon umbrella cocktails to moving scuba diving out of a cruise ship, building sandcastles to collecting sea shells. Life's a beach capsule contains everything. With this cartridge it's likely to enjoy all the cool things which you enjoy about the beach and summer, and each the things you like about scrapbooking and card making from the comforts of your own home!

The fresh life is a beach cricut cartridge is totally packed with the alphabet and characters made within an egyptian tiki layout, to intriguing shapes of smiling turtles and turtles into exquisite designs of birds, plants of paradise and hibiscus blossoms and a lot more sea contours that may bring the tropical sunshine and beauty to any scrapbook, greeting card or any task you could imagine!

How fun can it's to decorate your living room or outside porch so that it may feel like a day at the beach every day. You are able to do this that you know using the life is a beach cricut cartridge utilizing using the cricut vinyl to cut out shapes or by simply creating a stencil and stenciling these intriguing shapes on your walls, or maybe on the cement floor, flower pots or curtains using floral paint.

Now it's possible for you to make really trendy party invitations with the"name words" feature and clipping the party title that has a pineapple umbrella drink attached? Wish to go over simple and fun? I just finished creating twenty invitations to acquire a beloved friend's retirement party using the life's a beach cricut cartridge. I was done in no time at all.

Why are you likely to a cruise, or have pictures from an

earlier cruise that stay in a box? This is the very best cartridge to design cruising videos. They possess the cruise ship, ship charms, borders in addition to the attribute"title words" that says bon voyage working with a cruise ship attached. Exactly how cool is that.

Remember you can cut letter and shape measurements around 5.5 around the cricut machine and 23 inches across the cricut expression. This cartridge works with cricut die cutting machines. And in the event you presently possess the cricut design studio, you can preview each the amazing capabilities. But I am warning you, you are likely to appreciate what you see, therefore just buy it and start having fun.

Now that summer time is winding down, kids back into college, you will be able to undergo all those pictures that you took on your vacation or day trips to the beach or lake, or even your child playing in a sand box, and start scrapbooking. The choices are endless and the sea and coast would be the restriction with this enjoyable in sun cricut capsule life is a beach.

You will find three versions of the cricut system, popular personal die cutters made by the provo craft company. With three great choices, it can be tough to decide which to buy. In the event you begin little and buy the very first personal electronics cutter? Or is the expression version worth the extra investment? How do the generate, the hybrid variant currently being exclusively provided by Michael's Craft Store, stand up against the other two machines?

In a number of ways, all three die cut machines will probably be the same:

All three versions are cartridge-based. It's possible to just create cut-outs determined by the capsules you have. Each cartridge comprises a keyboard overlay, which may be used in picking specific cuts. The cartridges are not machine-specific - they might be utilized in any of these 3 versions.

Fundamental performance of 3 machines is precisely the same. In the event you have the personal electronic cutter, then you will have no difficulty working on the cricut expression or create (and vice-versa). Why? The basic operation of three die cutters is the specific same.

Here is a quick rundown of the process. After plugging in the selected cartridge and corresponding keyboard overlay and turning into the machine, you are all set to start making die cuts. Materials, such as paper or cardstock, are put on a certain cutting mat, which can be then loaded to the device working with the media of a button. With a different press of the button, the selected design is chosen. All that's left is to select"cut". The machine does the rest of the job.

All three cricut machine variations use the exact same accessories. It had been noted that the capsules are not machine-specific, but additionally this can be true with the vast majority of the extra accessories. It is not significant which model you have - the replacement blades blades, different tools, such as the cricut spatula, and design studio software, might be used with just about any version. The 1 exclusion is the cutting edge mats. The machines require various sizes of the mats, and you want to get one that is compatible with your individual machine.

Now that you know the way the cricut machines are equally, you are probably wondering how they are different. They alter in several ways:

The attributes of die cuts created by every machine are somewhat different. The personal electronics cutter gets the capacity of making cut-outs which range from 1 inch to 5-1/2 inches in measurement, in half inch increments. The create can produce expire cuts ranging from 1/4 inch to 11-1/2 inches in measurement, in quarter inch increments. The expression supplies users the highest flexibility, making cut-outs from 1/4 inch to 23-1/2 inches in measurement, in quarter inch increments.

They size and weight of those machines vary. The personal electronics cutter and create are equally modest, portable machines. These models are fantastic for crafters who would rather take their tasks around the road, and create record designs and other jobs in category configurations. They are also suited for men and women that do not have a certain place in their home location aside for crafting, because these die cutters are easy to package up and put away in between

174

programs. The expression, on the other hand, is much heavier and larger. In the event you've obtained a crafting corner or space, and do not have the worries of moving it frequently, it's an excellent alternative.

The three cricut machine variations have different functions and manners. There are many unique modes and functions. By means of example, the game to page design will automatically correct the dimensions of the die cut based upon the size of the material packed from the system. The center stage function enables you to align with the cutting edge blade throughout the center of the material, so the cut is made of it. The expression machine receives the most flexibility far as the access to modes and functions. Next in line is that the create, and third place goes to the personal electronic cutter. More information are available regarding those modes and functions in the machine handbooks, which may be seen in pdf format on cricut.com.

The buy cost differs for every single variant. The personal electronics cutter has been the very inexpensive cricut cutter, with a suggested retail price of $299.99. The generate is $100.00 more, at $399.99, in addition to the rake is $499.99. Please bear in mind that all of 3 machines can be purchased at considerable savings. Many retailers run special sales or have a lesser standard cost in comparison to proposed retail price. It's an excellent idea to shop around when buying your very first cricut machine.

Getting Your Cricut Mat Sticky Again

Can you know you do not need to buy a new mat every-time your mat discounts it's stickiness?

When your mat goes to the point at which nothing will stick anymore together with your paper only goes around when you try to cut, and then now is the time to"re-stickify" (is that a term??) Your mat. This is a very simple process and you're going to be amazed at how well it works!

• step 1- carry your mat in your sink. Use some hot water, a few drops of dish soap and a green scotch brite scrubbing pad. Scrub your mat under the tepid water. You will start to locate the tiny pieces of paper and filthy tacky dirt start to come off. You will possibly use the scrapper that came in your own cricut tool kit which will aid you scrap off a few of the gunk too. Keep scrubbing until all that extra layer of gunk is gone. Depending upon your mat, this may strip it all the way into the plastic with no stickiness left or there can nevertheless be a tiny bit of stickiness. Either way would be fine.

• measure 2- then you want to allow it airdry or use your own hair dryer. Don't use a towel to scrub it because it will leave lint behind.

• step 3- permit which airdry for about 1 hour. It's prepared to rock & roll again. I have done this in my mats and repeatedly.

- measure 4- then have a broad tipped zig 2 way glue pen and utilize paste in lines across the whole mat.

- step 5- let that dry for 1 hour before implementing the translucent sheet on top.

I have utilized other adhesives with this specific same way, but the zig 2 way pen is the adhesive I liked the ideal. It leaves your mat tacky, but maybe not as sticky as it was when it was new. Just perfect!!

I will say nevertheless, there'll come a stage the moment your mat does need to be retired. When the benefits begin curling up, it will influence the manner it rolls through the system.

In involving your "re-stickifiying", you might use baby wipes or a lint roller to remove lint and gentle dirt.

**please be cautious that this will invalidate your manufacturer guarantee on your cricut machine. Having said that, the warranty on your cricut is only for one year, therefore in the event you've had it longer than 1 year, it won't matter anyway.

Cricut scrapbooking - it's all about investments

Has anyone tried seeing a screen full of scrapbooks? It is a breath taking experience I tell you! When you have a peek at the high caliber and substances that the scrapbooks are made of, you might feel that the number of work and dedication that the creators of these scrapbooks wore just to be able to create them real. That is the main reason folks have a look at the craft of making scrapbooks because a very complex and fragile method that needs a lion's center together with a great deal of patience and dedication. It is not a easy process as you will have to conceptualize the strategy and make it. You simply need to envision what fat our ancestors had to undergo to simply have the capability to come up with one record. Now, but in case you take a look about you and inspect how things are moving together with the scrapbook world, so much has changed. Now let's talk cricut scapbooking.

When you input a screen of scrapbooks and you examine the recent ones, you are going to understand how amazing the designs of them are. You look at them and you begin to ask yourself the way that they could develop individuals and above all the way that they could create the plan concrete. The solution is actually simple.

If you would like to excel in the craft of scrapbooking, you desire a cricut cutting platform together with a software program. Nearly everyone owns a computer so I will not dig too much into that. However, with both above mentioned tools, those are requisites. The program tool is quite much the source of the designs. A very notable cricut scrapbooking app is the cricut design studio. Many scrapbook makers use this since it has a range of layouts that are jazzy which could match any scrapbook producer's preferred theme! After the design has been chosen, you then instruct your computer or laptop to decrease the design via your circuit cutting machine.

The cricut cutting machine is pretty much in control of cutting the design that you select from the cricut studio application. 1 cent cutting machine can cost you about $300 and it is worth every cent that you spend so please do not possess any second thoughts of buying one.

So constantly bear in mind the world of cricut scrapbooking is all about investments both in money and in efforts. It is about psychological fortitude. Consequently, in the event you don't own it, then state your ideas. This may be not the easiest thing to do yet the advantages might be enticing. I wouldn't have any second thoughts if I were you.

Cricut Sale - Improving Your Abilities

If a guy was great in something, would he do it free of price? From time to time, the answer will probably be"yes". But if it is a skill that you feel can provide food on the table you'll have to capitalize on it. Consequently, in the event you've got a cricut cutting instrument, a program, and a knack for handling designs and layouts, then this might be an opportunity for you to step up and start earning. This is where you'll discover a cricut sale.

The cricut machine could possibly be employed to lower the designs that you select in the software tool. With assistance from the cricut design studio, you will eventually discover the design that you look for a lot of stuff. However, before we proceed any further with the notion of approaches to obtain a cricut sale, let us understand the several applications of the layouts and patterns that we get from our software.

Greeting cards are one of the most common things that the designs are employed for. The cover is the most likely recipient of these designs or patterns. Consequently, in the event that you now have a theme in mind; plug in your computer, trigger the software and hunt to your design. If the cover deals with a Christmas theme subsequently hunt for design that will inform the story of Christmas. It is that easy. Consequently, in case you understand those who want their current cards then this is the most opportune time for you let the business individual in you speak.

The generation of calendars is still another superb undertaking that you can take part in utilizing all of the designs and patterns that come out of your software. Utilize the designs to breathe life into each month along with the design/s that you pick. If we are talking about december, then pick designs that have a christmas theme to it. Last but not least, one of the most common applications of this program patterns and designs are offered on decorations for walls. There aren't any limits to what you can do this the key is to just allow your imagination go mad on what decoration you will create.

So there you have it. When you learn the craft of creating the three that were just mentioned, you will have a cricut sale very fast. But obviously, you will need endurance and determination to create this work.

Crafters and scrapbook lovers like their cricut die cutting machines. With the arrival of the cricut picture, which cuts and prints art elements from numerous mediums, there is nearly no paper project you can not manage with cricut merchandise. Today we'll know how to properly keep your cricut cutting mats to prolong the life length of their mats and spare you a great deal of cash from the process.

Even though the cricut machines are not in any way challenging to maintain there are a range of things which you wish to learn to keep your cutting machine working on this tip top shape. Probably the most critical thing which you could do is make sure the cutting mats remain clean, undamaged, and possess the appropriate adhesive properties essential to keep your art medium on the mat.

To receive a speedy review it is vital to remember that the adhesive mat is something which holds your newspaper while is fed past the filler head, also at the case of the cricut picture the printer thoughts. Without a sticky mat the paper could change round from the machine as opposed to be cut or printed properly.

Today's an excellent time to also remind you that the mat

does not permanently keep its stickiness and sometimes has to be adjusted. So it is easy to understand that another benefit of correctly maintaining the cutting edge mat is that their lifespan is considerably increased which means you would like to buy them frequently hence the mat is an essential, but often overlooked, part of cricut machines.

Fundamental care includes cleaning, review, and proper storage. Once you complete with your cricut cutting mat inspect it for tears, tears, and gouges. When debris and gunk starts to grow on your mat just wash it with dish soap and warm water. Do not scratch it off or use any cleaning chemicals. Permit the mat to wash before you put it to storage. In between washings wipe down the mat using a lint free rag or a swifter sweeper sheet. Do these things and you may significantly increase the life span of your mat.

After your own cricut mats loose their stickiness today is the time to use a paste to make them survive much longer. You will find a terrific deal of mats available on the market you might attempt, but be forewarned many are ways to sticky to utilize to a cutting mat. A lot of people report excellent success with crafters companion others use stampin up stampin spray to add stickiness to elderly mats.

Before you include any adhesive to your own mats consistently be certain and wash the mat of any debris. Then wash with soap and warm water as explained above and allow to completely dry.

182

All all these are the principles of cricut cutting mat maintenance that will extend the life of your mats and save you a lot of cash. Play them clarified and you along with your cricut cutter will be a great deal happier.

Obtaining To Knows This Intricate Procedure

Everyone can appreciate what a great picture can do for you. Whenever you take a look at a stunning shot which you took let's state a few years back through your kid's high school graduation, you might see just what I mean. You study this movie and it seems just like you are teleported back in time and back to the graduation of your kid and you start to relive it. Pictures can speak a million words evoke a sea full of emotions. As a consequence of technology and what linked, we're able to conserve every exceptional moment we'd in manner or in motion. Cricut scrapbooking also has an integral part inside this.

The process of getting scrapbooks's been around for quite some time and this is considered a very meticulous process. You see, people revere scrapbook making as an art and a better method of keeping pictures. The materials and graphics are selected carefully so that they may endure the tests of time. In the event you produce a wonderful scrapbook, chances are it'll endure for decades and your great grandchildren's grandchildren will be able to watch and relive each second that their grandparents had. Now's not that something?

The process for scrapbook building has been made more convenient and faster thanks to the cricut cutting machine. The cricut cutting tool is a cricut scrapbooking tool that is responsible for cutting on the designs that you specify. When you pick the layout for your scrapbook, the first thing that you want to always put under consideration is the motif. If the pictures that are likely to be put by your scrapbook centers on a reunion that you had with your nearest and dearest then think about a design which will magnify the motif.

Back in the day, after you had finalized the design, another challenge you'll face now is the best way to produce the design. There is another tool which alleviates on your burden with this and that is the cricut design studio. This bad boy is a software program that has hundreds of hundreds of designs inside which you might choose from.

I guarantee you that you are going to be able to locate anything using this specific software application. 1 other fantastic thing about this app is that it supplies the user of the app the capacity to edit the designs and to make brand-new ones. Now that is technology at its very best.

So that's cricut scrapbooking to you!

How to find cheap cricut machines and discount cartridges

Cricut machines and cartridges could locate somewhat expensive if you don't shop around. In the event the buy price is holding you back, then rest assured we'll make it possible for you to acquire some amazing reductions and earnings.

The cricut expression machine, together with the very first are alike a dream come true for album lovers and paper craft lovers. You are in a position to make print, and then die cut any kind you'll be able to consider readily and easily. Just push a button and watch it operate, no computer required. Scrapbook designs, custom greeting cards, party decorations, and a lot more are made simple, easy, and quick using provo craft's new machine. With over 55 cricut cartridges to choose from, there's not any absence of occupation ideas you could invent.

The 1 disadvantage to these machines is the price. They save time and money, yet to start they require a hefty price of $299 to the personal cricut cutting machine and roughly $499 to your larger expression machine. This is in fact a hit anybodies pocket book.

Cartridges too are extremely pricey. These include the fonts, shapes, and various designs that you can create your system printing. Nevertheless every add-in cartridge normally costs around $50 all the way up to $100. Insert that on the first expense of your cricut and you've got a huge investment! Sure you will make money with your scrapbooking, it might pay for itself time and money saved, and lots of owners swear it's worth every dollar spent, but the initial payment is just too high for many.

The simplest way to find discount earnings on cheap cricut product would be to shop around. Shop the earnings in the regional craft stores like Micheal's and Joann fabrics. If there aren't any earnings coming soon, then you can always search online. We are big fans of buying our products out of ebay since you can discover some amazing discounts. Many times that the auctions are for whole bundles of capsules and a machine. Sometimes they throw in free bonus fittings to sweeten the deal. You will find both new and used machines for substantially below the sticker cost.

CHAPTER THREE
UNDERSTANDING CRICUT REWARDS

C ricut rewards are excellent because they specifically target saying and silhouette cutting machine clients. We love our private artwork cutters and are continuously purchasing several types of equipment like cricut vinyl. Vinyl has become quite popular due to its simplicity of usage, number of colours and quantity of lengths and sizes. As a good deal of us are extremely price conscious, we want the best value when purchasing cricut supplies. Reward software help reduce our overall cost of the supplies while demonstrating our loyalty to customer friendly businesses which produce a consistent efforts to recognize our purchases.

Vinyl cricut rewards are much more specific and valuable. Since vinyl has many applications from the craft marketplace, cricut vinyl sellers are rewarding their customers with innovative discounts depending on the sum of the purchases and their own consistency. Some vinyl cricut suppliers provide affiliate programs that benefit customers for promoting and advertising their particular cricut vinyl provide websites to their partners and friends. Everyone enjoys a fantastic deal and what deal is far better than free vinyl for your cricut. Sharing requires time and effort to get this a wonderful benefit.

Sophisticated cricut vinyl distribution organizations are supplying credits for their clients that are ready to share. Credits are created as cricut users upload and display their own particular cricut files they have made utilizing cricut vinyl. This process is actually a win- win assisting to lower the total price of vinyl supplies and helping to market the cricut plastic supply company as a commendable resource for further cricut users to obtain their vinyl materials. Businesses with eyesight are implementing cricut reward applications and will continue to create long term win-win relationships with their clientele.

Cricut cartridges make scrapbooking fun and straightforward

You have very likely noticed the pleasure with regard to cricut merchandise. Their level of flexibility and popularity are producing the cricut a legend within the scrapbooking and paper crafting world. Cricut is your private cutting system that doesn't have to get a computer.

Its cartridge-based system allows you to cut hundreds of stunning layouts, styles, and phrases in many different styles using only the touch of a button. Cricut typeface and shape cartridges set a number of their best layouts, letters, and phrases created by top scrapbook creative designers at the ends of your fingers.

Assessing out which cricut products you will want and want will be helpful once you begin in working with this incredible product!

Which cricut products will I probably must have?

In the time you purchase your cricut own electronic dispenser, you can expect to get the gear, a shapes cartridge alongside a cutting mat that will assist you begin. Immediately after figuring out ways to use the machine, yet, you're going to undoubtedly be prompted to obtain extra cricut items, probably beginning with additional cricut cartridges.

There are truly a multitude of those cricut cartridges readily available for sale, and they include a range of topics, fonts, and layouts. Your cricut machine employs unique cutting blades and cutting mats which might want to go replaced following numerous applications. Lots of extra optionally available cricut goods are sure to tempt your creativity in addition to that. Cricut supplies exclusive paper, cardstock, along with vinyl sheets, and you could also buy exceptional inks for use while using this machine.

Cricut organizational items such as the storage container, carrying luggage, and messenger bag can help keep your cricut tools organized and easy to transport. These accessories will surely be available wherever cricut products are available for sale, and they can surely be purchased to the cricut.com online website.

The Ideal Way to Purchase Cricut merchandise:

Cricut products are now commonly accessible through many distinct providers. Significant series hobby outlets will be sure to have a substantial assortment of cricut cartridges. Lower cost retail chain retailers also generally give you some cricut cartridges, even though you may have a little bit of trouble looking for each of the cartridges you are considering.

Neighborhood scrapbooking retail outlets an internet scrapbooking provide retailers will also provide cricut cartridges. Online auction sites, such as ebayare a wonderful resource for locating new cricut cartridges at a lowered price!

Registering your very own cricut merchandise:

It is an excellent concept to enroll your cricut products on the cricut site. Cricut goods are meticulously manufactured from the best top quality elements. At case that you have no problem with your cricut merchandise, nevertheless, provo craft includes a limited warranty.

Registering your very own cricut goods will certainly be certain you have implemented the actions required in the function that you may want to make utilization of this warranty. What's more, in the event you will discover in any given instant any kind of recognized problems or issues using cricut products, provo craft may have your current contact info to alert you.

Cricut tips - craft ideas for the cricut cutting machine

Wish a few cricut tips to your cricut cutting machine? Cricut private electrical cutters are revolutionizing hand crafts and individuals throughout the nation are astonished at the quantity of lovely and innovative things they can suddenly make.

The way a cricut works is straightforward: simply load among several available cartridges to the cutter, select what colour card stock you would really like to use for that specific layout and cut away. Each cartridge has plenty of themed layouts - whatever in seasonal layouts to favorite superheroes - and cricut users may pick one or more designs from each cartridge. The cut out designs are then stuck on...

Wall hangings

Scrapbooks

Picture frames

Custom greeting cards you name it everything's potential with a cricut.

Perhaps the very endearing cricut craft notion is a calendar. Another page can be made for every month, and each of these different pages can be decorated with several designs. July, for example, will soon be trimmed with the layouts within this freedom day seasonal cartridge while february is the clear choice for the love struck seasonal cartridge. The fun doesn't end there, but alongside the mother's day cartridge is going to be ideal for may while the easter cartridge is a natural for april. December is unique is cricut-land, and cricut customers have a good deal of collections of layouts like the joys of the season cartridge and the snow friends cartridge to select from.

What can life be without scrapbooks to record each and every waking moment of the most prized possessions: our children? Together with the cricut cutting platform, scrapbooks could be personalized to each and every child, and what might be better in comparison to mother and child - or dad and kid - to repay together and select which pictures they'd love to decorate their own graphics with. Cricut also knows that boys and girls are distinct and that, although the boys probably will not like using the once upon a princess cartridge, they'd go mad over the batman: the brave and the bold cartridge. Small women, on the other hand, would likely turn their flavorful wake up at the robotz cartridge but might love the disney tinker bell and friends cartridge. You'll never be at a loss for cricut scrapbooking ideas.

Your cricut design ideas are not only restricted to pictures, however, and alphabets are also available - such as the sesame street font cartridge in addition to all the ashlyn's alphabet cartridge - them will come in handy when it is time to customize a present. Ideal presents would include images of critters - or maybe vinyl wall-hangings commemorating a special occasion like that excursion overseas - all, of course, adorned with bright and beautiful cricut cutouts. Cricut caters to every eventuality, and, here, the create a critter cartridge in addition to the summer in Paris seasonal cartridge is going to be ideal to suit you cricut home decoration.

Birthdays, graduations, Christmas, Hanukkah, bar mitzvahs, baby showers: the present list is endless and this doesn't include those tasks that are finished"just for fun". Cricut has capsules to suit each and every event - and each and every project - that is considered. Completing a cricut task jointly is also a superb way to find a family to bond, along with the stunning things that are made jointly could be cherished for a lifetime.

With a cricut personal electric cutter just the heavens - and your imagination - is your limit.

What you need to learn about the cricut personal cutter before you purchase

Before purchasing your hard earned cash to some die cutting platform, you must do your own study. There are numerous models available on the industry and after much consideration that this is the one I have selected and why.

The cricut personal cutter device produced by provocraft is a wonderful edition to your scrapbooking tools. There are a few different cricut personal cutters. The cricut expressions will reduce 12x 24 inch dimension papers. The cricut original cuts 6x12 inch paper. The cricut cutting mat includes a gentle adhesive and retains your paper set up although the cutting is done. Each cricut machine involves a cartridge, the cricut original contains george & basic shapes and it is a fundamental cartridge, which combines capital lettering named george and a choice of shapes. Each cartridge consists of capsule, a keypad overlay and a few include an instruction booklet. So as soon as you've got unpacked your new cricut personal cutter you will have the ability to start experimenting immediately away. Down the screen you further expand the operation of your cricut system, along with other cricut capsules. Provocraft is publishing new cricut cartridges annually and they have wide assortment of topics, from alphabets, sports, in the garden via to disney characters.

On the cricut personal cutter you will have the ability to adjust blade depth, cutting and pressure speed. This assists when cutting different materials. Slowing down the cutting edge speed provides a far better result with much more fragile scrapbooking paper, although using medium pressure provides a crisper cut scrapbooking cardstock rather than the softest anxiety setting.

You can cut shapes and letters by adjusting the measurements dial from 1 around 5 1/2 inch. The sizes available are 1, 11/4, 11/2, 2, two 1/2, 3, 31/2, 4, 41/2, 5, 51/2.

The capability to load the scrapbooking paper, then cut a

couple of letters, then unload the newspaper and reload to exactly the point you'd been around, saves time and newspaper.

The cricut cartridge George and basic shapes contains six innovative capabilities. Signal, slotted, charm, silhouette, shadow and shadow blackout.

Signal - imagine a picket sign using a lien or silhouette cut out

Slotted - oval ring, a slot cut in the best to thread ribbon or twine

Charm - your correspondence or form cut using a circle attached on top, so you can join the correspondence using a brad to your design

Silhouette - cuts the outline of your correspondence or form. Great for the budget conscious as you are in a place to maintain the negative cut of your letter and use it on a different design.

Shadow - cuts the letters or shapes, somewhat large than normal, these can subsequently be used behind the standard size letter, giving the appearance of a shadow along with a 3d effect for your name. This attribute is on every of these cricut cartridges.

Shadow blackout - like darkness except where there are a cut in the middle of a o for instance, shadow blackout simply generates the outdoor shadow with no cutout within the o

With this a variety of cricut capsules accessible, you wish to appear into the qualities of every one before your purchase, to make certain you will get sufficient use from each investment. Consider if they provide just shapes or shapes and decoration. I've obtained a few shapes capsules and since the contours were so complex, I wasn't particularly bothered that Christmas cheer cricut cartridge did not arrive using an alphabet. The Christmas cheer capsule is just one I would not be without.

Provocraft additionally, it released a stronger cutting blade, which might cut about 1.5 millimeter thickness. This usually means that all the provo cricut personal cutters, employing this brand new blade, can cut chipboardvinyl, vinyl, cloth and magnetic sheets.

Cricut suggestions - tips on how to make the most of your own cricut machine

The cricut machine was made for a great number of factors. Now most folks may believe that this gadget is only for producing scrapbooks but it is not. The cricut machine may be used for whole lot more of things than simply creating scrapbooks. Should you look closes in a cricut machine and you allow your creativity go crazy, you can think of a whole lot of great cricut ideas that could allow you to have a source of simple or living give your individual satisfaction.

196

As what was cited previously, people associate the use of a cricut machine with just making scrapbooks. One of the superb cricut ideas which are worth sharing is a cricut machine may also be employed to make splendid calendars. The cricut machine in addition to the cricut design studio software could possibly be utilized to produce designs for your own calendar.

One calendar season is constituted of 12 weeks. Take note that every month consistently has a theme for this as becoming wet, cold, and there can even be weeks that are notable for a particular occasion. With all the two tools which we just mentioned, it is possible to make and pick designs that might breathe life into a particular month. Let utilize the whole month of December for example. December is closely connected with winter and Christmas. If we were to make a cricut calendar depending on the month of december, then you want to select designs which could mirror this season. Some amazing designs for this month contain reindeers, snowmen, and Santa clause himself. That's so cool wouldn't you say?

In addition into a cricut calendar, the cricut cutting machine might also be utilized to make your private gift cards. When you visit malls or to shop that concentrate on selling cards, I am pretty much certain you'll always be longing for another layout. With the usage of cricut machine along with the attempts from the cricut style studio, you may produce your gift card with your design and no one will prevent you. You're your own boss.

Selecting the ideal cricut for you

Before you purchase your first cricut, it is important to consider all probable choices to choose the best machine to coincide with your crafting needs.

First, you have to stock up to the principles, such as cricut ribbon and image capsules. These capsules may come in many different subjects to showcase and commemorate any event, like vacations, vacations or forthcoming events. You'll also take a large quantity of coloured paper together with a pad on that to decrease that contrasts into the size of your system.

If you're a avid scrapbooker, you ought to check into buying a first cricut cutter or the cricut expression. This system will cut shapes, themes and letters to decorate your scrapbook pages. It is also possible to decorate bulletin boards, posters, party decorations, greeting cards or invitations of any type. The cutters may also lessen cloth too. It's encouraged that you starch the fabric first so as to generate the task as simple as possible for your system to complete. The difference between the two is straightforward. The cricut expression is a brand new, 12" x 24" version of the first cricut. This program makes it easier to create large-scale jobs at a huge amount - if you have got the ideal quantity of paper. Font and picture cartridges can be utilized from the 2 machines.

Have you heard of the cricut cake? This helpful cutter is designed to cut almost anything for baked products, such as frosting sheets, gum paste, fondant, cookie dough, tortillas, baking soda, gum and the majority of other soft food materials. Whatever material you decide to use should be involving 1/16" and 1/8" thick. Maintain the blade clean continuously so as to guarantee the very best cut possible.

Another popular cricut alternative is your cricut cuttlebug. This system is small. It merely cuts paper that's 6 inches wide and weighs just 7 pounds. The cuttlebug is principally used for cutting and embossing particular crafts. Here is the very best method to decorate several greeting cards invitations. Once you add a range of colored expires, then the cuttlebug is going to be prepared to emboss immediately. These dies are also harmonious with Sizzix, big shot and thin cuts machines, which serve a similar purpose.

Why are you interested and creating your own personal t-shirts and fabric layouts? Cricut also created the Yudu for those crafters that love screen-printing and making their own layouts. The Yudu allows its owners to attach with some laser ink jet printer and earn a layout to screen-print onto practically anything! Yudus are used for straps, handbags, photo eyeglasses, shoes - you name it.

Finally, if you would like to feed your newfound cricut obsession, go right ahead and buy one of those newest cricut gypsys. This helpful, hand-held apparatus will keep your font cartridges for simple portable use. It's possible to design from anyplace on the move, in the physician's office, even while on holiday, or simply sitting on your sofa. Anything you intend on the gypsy is completely transferable to some cricut machine for cutting edge. If you save your design, it may be connected to some of your cricut devices and published at a later moment.

This is a succinct overview of a few of the cutting edge machines cricut sells. As you can see there is a fantastic assortment of machines for whichever specific sort of craft which you wish to focus on. 1 thing is for sure. Whichever machine you choose you will have many hours of inspiration and fun producing and creating your own crafting jobs.

Cricut Cutter - The Personal Die-Cutter

The cricut cutter by provo craft is a die-cutting machine utilized chiefly for scrapbooking and card making. Since the creation of the very first camera, in the 1830's that the increase of scrapbooking has increased exponentially. It's been an exciting and rewarding avocation for several years utilizing the cricut cutter making it much easier for the average individual to become creative.

There are several variations from the existing cricut cutter series: the (first) cricut personal electronic cutter; the cricut expression machine; cricut produce; as well as the cricut picture. They vary in price from $100.00 to $600.00

depending on the merchandise and accessories included. Components and various additional cartridges might be had separately.

The cricut personal electronic cutter requires no computer or applications and even though it's not a portable device it is lightweight and compact enough to take with you if you could go to celebrations, plants, or perhaps scrapbooking classes. Just plug it in, flip it, and also this small cricut is prepared to decrease numbers, shapes, and letters about 5.5" tall and around 11.5" long.

The cricut expression machine is a 24" private digital cutter and the most recent addition to the cricut cutter system. With two brand new cutting mats now you can cut numbers, shapes, letters, and personalities from 0.25" up to an impressive 23.5".with six brand new styles and several new functions you've got a bigger capacity to customize your cuts, as well as the new settings enable various units of measurement and languages. You are able to utilize present cartridges replacing the necessity to collect tens of thousands of heavy die cuts.

The cricut produce combines the portability of this very first cricut machine using the operation of the cricut expression. This machine in the cricut cutter show is precisely the same size as the first, yet permits cuts out of 0.25" around 11.5" onto a 6" x 12" cutting mat. This very small machine also exclusively offers the newest eight-way directional blade;

portrait mode will reduce taller images, and also lots of other new ways to boost the performance of this machine. The enhanced screen and ultra-sleek layout add increased style and simplicity.

With this lineup of cricut cutter, the cricut expression and picture have been designed for those that have a crafting corner or space, where you don't have the worries of going frequently for it is bigger and thicker. The cricut personal electronic cutter and cricut produce are smaller, streamlined, more aerodynamic machines and also have a convenient travel bag. These models are appropriate for people who don't have a certain location in their house location aside for crafting, like to take their tasks to a families or friend home, enjoy creating or teaching document layouts and other jobs in class configurations, or needs to put away between programs. It's possible to utilize the cricut cutter on your classroom, office, home or at even begin your own scrapbooking business.

Amazing Cricut Card Suggestions For The Nearest and Dearest

Why spend another cent on a store bought greeting card now which you've got a cricut cutting apparatus. You paid a lot for this cricut, so let us put it to function. Listed below are just a few cricut card ideas which can get you started and allow you to use any of your cricut capsules you decide on.

The following holiday coming on the calendar is Easter. While I think about everything cricut card ideas I can come up with, I think about your loved ones members and friends will respond if they receive a handmade greeting card created by you. Now that you've got your cricut cutting machine alongside many different cricut capsules, it is really simple to add your own personal signature into a card.

If one of the cricut cartridges you've got is the cricut doodlecharms cartridge, you may produce a really adorable handmade greeting card in the easter bunny or a easter basket filled with colored eggs. Or another among those cricut cartridges is your cricut wild card cartridge so it's likely to generate a filigree easter egg card. One of my cricut card thoughts is if you have obtained the cricut stretch your imagination cartridge. You can produce a card with a bunny coloring Easter eggs or perhaps a bunny in a basket.

As much as all the cricut card thoughts I could develop for Easter, not these need to possess bunnies or eggs . Here's a fantastic example of working with another one of the cricut capsules known as a walk in my garden capsule. With this cricut cartridge you're in a position to produce amazing daffodil, hyacinth, or tulip are the subject of your card. You are the artist of this Easter card, show your creativity and have fun.

Subsequently the upcoming significant card day is mothers day. Consider how your mother will feel obtaining a handmade greeting card out of her small one. You may absolutely make her day. Whatever cricut cartridges you've you are going to have the ability to acquire something that will put a grin on her face, not to mention you may do this all with your glorious cricut cutting machine. It may be as simple as a simple blossom out of the planting schoolbook cartridge, so which you simply cut into a variety of sizes and coating onto a card, then put in the words happy mothers day, or to the very best mommy around earth.

The good thing on your cricut cutting machine and nearly all of the cricut cartridges which are readily available for you is that it provides you a large number of cricut card thoughts. You are going to see your cards appear so professional you will not have the ability to wait to ship them out or start selling them. I can get busy making my greeting cards on my cricut cutting machine, how about you?

What is the cricut picture machine?

The cricut picture machine, declared by provocraft at the craft & hobby association summer convention and tradeshow (cha) is merely one of its kind. It's now the only machine which lets the user to cut and publish using precisely the same apparatus, saving a great deal of money and time. Featuring inkjet printing technologies by hp, you opt for a layout from a broad library of capsules, and have it published and than cut one go.

However, what does it mean to scrapbookers?

The use of cutouts and shapes in a variety of colours are a great way to enhance and add pizzazz to a variety of crafts and arts projects, such as scrapbooking and card making.

All these additionally known as diets might be of a myriad of substances, including card stock, vellum, lean plastics, foils and transparencies.

With nearly all of manual and digital cutters available on the market nowadays, like the sizzix and cricut expression, you need to plan ahead of time and select the color of your die-cut prior to cutting. To put it differently, the color of your style will be the color of this paper (or fabric, or inventory) you pick.

In as a result, when creating complex or elaborate layouts, you may need to change paper colours frequently.

Added systems, such as the wish blade, let you print your preferred shape with a standard inkjet printer than run onto the printed page through the system to reduce. The largest issue for this is that it's a two step process, using two distinct machines, which requires the consumer properly setup registration marks so that the machine will know just where to cutback. This is often a trial and error procedure and the results are not always satisfactory.

Thus, the requirement is present for a system that permits the consumer to publish a picture and lessen the image without manual registration. This is the point where the cricut picture comes in, to meet with a huge gap in the current market and open an entirely new world of possibilities for scrapbookers, cardmakers and paper crafters generally.

CHAPTER FOUR
MATERIALS TO USE WITH
CRICUT

C ricut jobs are some thing that you can do with your cricut cutting machine. It might be anything from simple activities that could provide you with private pleasure to people that may allow you to make revenue. Earlier, this system has been considered nothing but a scrap booker's tool. But with the expanding imagination of humanity, ideas are growing and growing like angry.

People want to realize that the cricut cutting machine is merely a die cutting tool also it is not the one that is directly accountable for the creation of those designs. The designs can be found via applications cartridges and resources. All that cricut machine does is that it dismisses the designs that the user chooses in the capsules or applications and not anything more.

The software that is responsible for producing layouts for your many cricut tasks is the cricut design studio. This bad boy has hundreds and hundreds of designs that you are able to select from. Furthermore, you might even create your own design and edit those that are within their library. When you have decided on your layout, have the cricut machine trimming out it and you are good to go for prime time.

Greeting cards is 1 task that the cricut machine could possibly be used for. Lots of individuals have their own layout they've conceptualized and imprinted unto their own heads. Nearly all the time, the mall that you see will not have the design that you're looking for. Sometimes they may but that's a leap of faith. Along with the cricut system, you might create your own design and be delighted with that.

In addition, you're in a position to market these cards that you create and generate income. Today that's company man's mindset for you! This motion will help alleviate frustration and tension and permit you to accomplish a level of calmness or comfort.

Calendars may also be a consideration. Calendars have 12 months annually and each of those months have their own identity. With assistance from a cricut cutting edge system, you're in a position to help give life to those months. Make sure you produce or chosen designs which might help paint the mood of the month or whatever's linked with that.

Invitations are also exceptional cricut jobs. You pick a design that's acceptable for the occasion and after that you have made it cut through the cricut cutting machine. The trick is never to allow you imagination relax. Make sure you keep it going and you'll have more jobs function on.

The cricut machine has been known as a"scrap booker's

best friend". Following the process for scrapbooking was relatively new to the entire world as well as the general public, things were not always smooth sailing. Every scrap booker required to go through the tedious process of thinking up the strategy. When that was completed, people had to cut the design in order that they could place it to the scrapbook.

The cutting-edge part was the toughest and most compulsory hands which weren't capable of making any mistakes. That point from the scrapbooking world is history on account of this cricut cutting machine. With this excellent instrument, you may surely do a lot of things like cricut tasks that could be for your own personal gratification or for company related purposes.

One of the very usual cricut tasks is clearly scrapbooks. Scrapbooks are a great way to preserve memories. At any time you've got a pair of pictures that share a universal and ordinary motif such as birthdays, weddings, birthdays and so many more, you will turn into scrapbooks to guarantee those moments are relived.

You have to produce designs which may assist the audience feel the atmosphere that is being portrayed. You conceptualize, pick the program in the cartridge or applications and have it trimmed via a cricut machine. In the event you have people who have to have layouts cut to get their scrapbook, then they can always turn for one to have it done. That are a wonderful potential for some money.

Greeting and greeting cards are also excellent jobs for your cricut cutting machine. Whenever you take a look at a calendar, then it is 12 weeks indoors. It's possible to utilize the cricut cutting machine to cut designs from your software that might help portray the whole month which you select. Let's consider for example the month of February. February is connected with love since valentine's day happens on the 14th.

You can choose designs that are filled with hearts and anything has to do with love. In the event of greeting cards, you might use the cricut system to cut back designs that you pick. Sometimes the design that you look for in a greeting might just be discovered in your system so that you're so much better off doing so via cricut machine.

All these are cricut tasks which will be able to enable you to exude satisfaction and gain at the specific same instant. Do not stop with these ideas. The vital issue is to innovate.

Your scrapbook designs could be significantly improved by detecting attention-getting titles. A amazing method to do this is to begin with a plentiful supply of scrapbooking alphabets. As a good deal of us aren't delighted with our own handwriting and we're constantly watching out for alternatives, here are a couple which make a wonderful start.

First, how do you have to get your words in your page?

The easiest is to find a kind of writing you like and practice until you are happy with that. Otherwise it's a trip to the regional scrapbook shop to commit your hard earned money on alphabets - again!

So... Having loaded the dishwasher, the washing machine in addition to the drier, got the kids to school, made appointments into your dentist and the hair dresser for everyone, attended the pta meeting and obtained the supermarket for dinner, you merely have time between your lunch date with hubby and amassing the dry cleaning to run to the scrapbook store before it's time to collect the kids from school, provide them a snack cook dinner so it's ready once you return from soccer practice, then home again to eat dinner, help with homework, and get the kids to bed, and research some family problems with hubby before you hit the sack... Incidentally, if do you have got sufficient time to document?

Anyhow, at any time you do get it in the scrapbook store what exactly are you going to locate there?

You should encounter a humungous option of

· lettering stickers

· rub-ons

· die cuts

· stamps

· duration and duration embellishments

Any of them can create excellent titles, journaling and ideas on your layouts.

Let us take a peek at some of them...

Alphabet decals

All these come in most shapes, sizes, colors, fonts and materials - cardstock, bubbles, jelly, pebbles, to mention but a few. They are extremely easy to use and will add colour and fun to your scrapbooking layouts.

The drawback is they never seem to include adequate letters and you might just produce a few words in the specific same fashion. It's possible, but use leftover letters as'drop capitals' at the beginning of paragraphs in your own journaling. You can get off with different unique fashions such a fashion. And also a couple of layouts permit you to mix and match specific fashions inside the title or bullets for example. It's interesting to add random fashion characters at the center of the journaling, too.

Rub-ons

All these were known as transports when I was a kid, and only came as letters. They come as words or letters and phrases in an range of colors, and many beautiful layouts, too.

Since the name suggests, you simply rub them onto your own page with the very small rod supplied. (it's possible to use a bone folder or perhaps a coin if you eliminate the pole.) It's an excellent idea to lower across the words which you would love to use and put them carefully or you may find stray pieces from the word next door you had not meant to move.

Rub-ons look excellent, and offer a professional finish.

Alphabet stamps

All all these are a wonderful buy as you're in a position to steer clear of this'never-have-all-the-letters-i-need' syndrome that happens with various sites - plus they are re-useable!

It is easy to pin phrases together with replicate letters should you opt for stamps. Simply line up the letters onto a translucent acrylic block to form your expression, leaving the proper size place to the replicate letters which you put in on the following pass.

To rescue the ideal gap, put another postage in the place where the letter belongs, and the moment you have completed the word remove it and you're left with a space where you pinpoint the letter afterwards. It's likely to pinpoint the letters properly since it's possible to determine where you are stamping. After use, just wipe clean, replace the sheet and they're ready for next time!

Additional decoration antiques

You will find chipboard letters, metal letters, punched letters, self adhesive letters, button letters, brad letters, scrabble letters, paper tile letters; alphabets in a variety colors, fabrics, and... You name it, you can probably get it! You will encounter a great deal of fascinating accents to check in your scrap booking pages.

Mechanical and electronic systems

The various die cutting system apps have some excellent alphabets, butif you are new to scrapbooking they might appear a costly technique to create your titles. The results are outstanding and well worth the expense if you think you are going to also use some of the a range of unique shapes on the market. You will get outstanding use from them particularly in case you produce your own greetings cards, too.

Some titles to watch out for are sizzix, big shot, quickutz, cricut and xyron, to mention but some.

You can even buy a set of ribbon punches.

What is left?

But, before making the trip to the regional scrapbooking store contemplate utilizing your pc. You now have many fonts onto it and you will find a lot more available to download free from the internet.

Your computer is one of the most flexible practices to earn a journaling or name. With the massive selection of fonts you will find one that suits your design layout, but far more useful is the flexibility with regard to dimensions. It's possible to find the font as large as you want to acquire a title, or small enough to obtain all your journaling onto a tag.

You may conserve a whole lot of money with the guidance of your computer.

How can you get titles from the pc to your design?

It is very uncomplicated and quick to execute.

· choose a font and size it appropriately to your project.

· type your phrases, then print using the inverse image setting on your printer options.

· transfer to the wrong side of your chosen pattern or color paper or cardstock,

· remove and follow your scrap book card or job.

If you don't have, or can't track down the contrary image setting, then:

· carefully follow on your phrases - a light box will help you to the perfect side of the paper,

· cut within your lines.

And there you have it.

It is fantastic to have hundreds of choices of alphabets for our layouts. However, do try to avoid having one fashion too often, as it is likely to be boring to make and also to observe a record full of the exact same designs.

Now you see how easy it is to make excellent names and journaling, there's nothing stopping you. Have fun creating your memories and will you have enough time to save them on amazing scrapbook designs.

Scrap-booking is the latest crafty phenomenon. With the coming of digital cameras, the traditional photo albums have gone by the wayside along with the better way to keep substantial photos and the memories linked. There are numerous programs for avid scrap-bookers from several papers, ribbons, stickers and shapes, can it not be great to have these goods in one central location and at the touch of a button? Cricut expression is your answer. This personal digital cutter enables you to produce a few of the very beautiful and customized shapes to add flare to a most basic of paper crafts.

Resembling a photo printer, the cricut helps you design and cut on beautiful and exceptional layouts to use in your scrap-booking jobs. Together with the capacity to earn shapes between 1/8th and 24 inches, it's excellent to get a scrap-booker that requires more control within their layouts. Concerning the paper, the cricut will function at any newspaper like card stock, vellum, and at times even chipboard.

The cricut is lightweight and is easily transportable for just about any scrap-booking bash. In the event you need to travel with it, then there is also a carrying case available, particularly created for travel and comes complete with wheels, cushioning and a handle. All you'll need is electricity and a passion for scrap-booking and the cricut will perform the task for you.

Now here's the best part - if you don't know how to use a computer, then the cricut will function on its own with a computer. The cricut takes capsules that contain all the information that the machine needs in order to cut unique shapes. Want more of shapes that are unique? Just get another cartridge and you might have literally thousands of shapes and fonts available.

If you do know how to use a pc, connecting it to your computer can allow it to become considerably more elastic than the device alone. You can get applications known as"sure cuts plenty" which lets you design your own designs, shapes and fonts and have the cricut perform the rest of the task by cutting it out to you. Along with the applications, there's absolutely not any limit to what you can design. In the event you've obtained the ideas, the sure cuts plenty applications can permit you to design it.

For those whined that a system can waste paper by not utilizing all the space available, don't worry. The cricut was created not simply to make wonderful fonts and contours, but it may take action in like fashion that will maximize the customer of the paper, which is going to continue to keep the number of waste to a minimum.

With a growing quantity of newspaper crafters using digital die cuts to create scrapbook pages, cards and decorations, and the impulse to comprehend how to import and decrease svg files on a cricut digital die cutting system is also rising.

Even novice scrapbookers do not feel intimidated by digital die cuts. The custom of archiving, archivingcutting and preparing the designs is in reality rather straightforward. And with two standard third-party software programs readily available on the marketplace (sure cuts a lot and make the cut), each with active message boards and assist forums, any glitches have to be easily solved.

First, anybody planning to utilize svg files should have three things: a cricut system (possibly the very first private"baby bug," that the generate or the 12-by-12-inch capable expression), using a regular printer cable along with sure cuts a lot or produce the cut.

Sure cuts plenty (scal) and produce sure cut (mtc) are easily available for sale through their respective makers. Scal may be utilized with both mac and pc, while mtc was designed for the two pcs and will only use a mac that is running boot camp as well as parallels.

Even though some sites make files available for sale, there are plenty of accessible free of price. You'll come across svgs out there in a variety of topics, from critters to holidays to toys. Many images are similar in quality to the designs available on the cricut capsules provided by provo craft for $70 to $80 each.

After you find a svg file that you need, download it to your pc. It's typically just a very simple procedure of clicking on a download button or link, then"unzipping" a compressed file by double-clicking on the record name once it's downloaded and then selecting extract. It's an excellent idea to organize your svg"set" into folders by subject, or via a different system.

If you're using sure cuts a lot, open the program and the mat screen will look. It is possible to put your electronic mat in to 12-by-12, 6-by-12 or perhaps 12-by-24, dependent on how large your cricut system together with real life mat. Under the file menu, then choose"publish svg" then navigate in the svg image and click ok to import it. You are going to be able to change the image's dimensions, rotate it and combine it with various images, among other functions.

In make the cut, start the program so the mat screen looks and choose"import," subsequently"svg/svgz document" the image is going to appear in your electronic mat and you're going to have the ability to pick"shape magic" and"split" the svg to split it at the regions of the picture.

In either program, the moment you have the elements of this image organized how you want them, normally by color and maximizing paper use, arrange your cardstock or paper in the corresponding areas of the tacky cricut mat.

Save your job, make confident the cricut mat is packaged into the device (assess blade strain and speed) and pick the"cut" command. In the event you have some difficulty, remember, both scal and mtc have occupied service communities.

Another benefits of using third party software with the cricut is the capability to decrease any true type font, for example welding (joining together) letters.

After that the layout is cut, it might be constructed with glue. Many paper crafters, along with people using svg designs for school projects, home decor or other applications, like to include dimension and their own creative spin to die cuts with white gel pens, chalk, ink, glitter glue or dimensional"pop" dots.

As many paper crafters who like saving money when enlarging their innovative options, applying designer cut files utilizing a cutter such as cricut is an easy method to master, as a consequence of premium quality svgs and third party software.

Even though the cricut design studio includes advantage after advantage, my personal preferred is the capability to incorporate images from a lot of capsules into one layout. The user may design together with the cartridge options concurrently rather than being limited to clipping with one cartridge in the specific same instant.

Advanced together with ultra-creative users have created lots inspiring tasks by mixing many different capsules into a extraordinary cutting edge.

The cricut design studio can also preserve my estimation, a necessity for every single cricut owner. Though there's a learning curve to find this, after it is understood the creative options are completely infinite. The cricut and all the design studio have become a must-have resource for every scrapbooker and card maker today.

Are you allergic to the cricut style studio?

1 disappointment to your customers is your cricut design studio is not mac compatible. At the moment, you might just use this app with windows xp or vista. The sole difficulty is that you are restricted to using design studio at a location in which you've got access to a pc. If you have got a laptop, however, that is a non-issue.

Generally, that the cricut layout studio is a great addition to a cricut collection. You are only limited by your own creativity.

One of the terrific benefits of possessing cricut design studio is your capability to collaborate with other people. Each guy who designs a record can save the record within their pc. Many elect to set the file online and allow various folks to utilize their designs also. The moment that you start browsing other people's occupation, you will be amazed at the incredible work of these generous and talented cricut users. Following is a step-by-step guide to downloading and cutting together with assorted people's files.

You are likely to come across different websites and sites that have jobs posted with the cutting edge records also. Each person could shop and go over their records in a different fashion. Most use a third party record sharing site, though others have the files hosted right there on their website. A number of these files on the cricut.com message board was saved as a text document and need to be changed prior to using.

When you've found a list you would like to utilize, you would like to initiate the download process.

1. Click the link they have provided for you to the record. When it is hosted on their website, it will ask you after you'd really like to begin, cancel or save. If the record is hosted on a file sharing site it will let you wait the to"click here to download record". When you select that link it will take you into the screen that asks from the contest you'd like to begin, saveor cancel.

2. When you are on the beginning or shop display, you are very likely to need to choose save. Before you are doing, make certain the record is showing the place that you want the record to be saved. You may elect to generate a folder specifically for cricut documents. If you would like to change the document name, then take action in this stage. Click here to begin saving the file for your pc.

The record is on your computer, it's quite likely to launch it within the cricut design studio program. Stick to these simple tasks to reduce a layout that is stored.

Easy Cricut Projects for Beginners

Easy iron on vinyl projects

One of the most basic cricut materials is iron on vinyl, also known as heat transportation plastic (as well as htv for short). Take a look at how to use cricut iron on vinyl post. It is all (and I mean everything!) You might ever want to know.

The most obvious alternative is using it on apparel. Take a peek at my using iron on vinyl on a top post for ideas on choosing vinyl, which makes it up, and making sure it sticksfor great!

Subsequently take a peek at another iron plastic jobs that are super simple for novices!

· iron on vinyl on a wood sign

· "don't moose with me" baby onesie

· constructing a banner with iron on vinyl on card stock

· sprinkle shoes

· customizable tooth fairy pouches

Easy adhesive vinyl projects

Glue vinyl is merely one more material that's fantastic for

newcomer cricut users. It's basically a massive decal! My easy personalized water bottles are an enjoyable undertaking. You might even take a look at my guide to using transport tape, along with layering adhesive vinyl.

Here are some adhesive vinyl jobs the new cricut user can produce!

· DIY Pantry Labels

· Wood Sign with Adhesive Vinyl

· Using Adhesive Vinyl within an Ornament

· Sprinkle Halloween Pumpkin

Easy Card Stock + Paper Projects

Card inventory and paper are only two of my favorite stuff for new cricut customers since they're so inexpensive --perfect as soon as you're starting out and don't want to dedicate a wonderful deal of money!

It is a lot of fun making cricut projects. You may make a variety of crafts together with your own cricut research or even cricut maker cutting machine. There are many great cricut ideas to try. Here you're going to see an increasing list of occupation tutorials, cricut information, tips, tools and testimonials. Whether you are a newcomer to cricut or some protracted time cricut customer, I hope you discover what you like.

Cricut project ideas

I 'm always discovering new designs and project ideas to make to your personal cricut machine. I like sharing ideas, if you consider something you think I might be able to design or you want to discuss something you've created, give me a shout! I love to find out what other women and men create using their cricut! There are as many cricut ideas since there are people, times that the number of materials you will have the ability to utilize. Whether you've obtained a cricut research (first, air or air 2) or you have a cricut maker, you may produce fantastic DIY tasks for almost any function.

Versatile vinyl.

From wall graphics and framed art to java fountains and fountains, vinyl is your quick and effortless system to make an impression. Choose a design, set your vinyl in a method, and press proceed. Produced with cricut machines within mind, cricut vinyl always delivers excellent results.

Immediate sewing jobs.

Cricut revolutionizes sewing craft projects using countless digital designs from top manufacturers like simplicity®, all immediately accessible for the production. Just a few clicks and cricut maker® cuts and marks all those pieces for your next stuffed animal or clutch. The sewing is left up to you.

Iron-ons with personality.

With a variety of colors, finishes, and effects, iron-on compounds are excellent for customizing t-shirts, scarves, cushions, bags, and much more. Cut a design, then use cricut easypress™ (or even a iron, even in case you want to) to utilize it to your project of choice. Quick and pleasurable, cricut iron-on is for everyone!

Worldly wall art.

You get an entirely new perspective on crafting as soon as you use the cricut knife blade™ to reduce materials like balsa wood, basswood, chipboard, and matboard about 2.4 mm thick (depending on the material). Fantastic for puzzles, skeletons, architectural models, wall art, and a lot more.

Paper crafts for every single function.

What better way to join the world of crafting compared to utilizing the first cricut material of choice: paper! Paper comes in a huge choice of colors, textures, weights, and finishes. Use it to get party decorations, table settings, paper flowers, cards, notes, plus a whole lot more.

Quilting reinvented.

Save precious time developing a traditional gift. Cutting quilt cubes with cricut maker is fast, easy, and true. Start with a digital quilt design from riley blake™, or upload your own. You may skip the problem of cutting those cubes by hand, and save the intriguing parts all on your own.

Spectacular stencils.

Versatile and easy, stencils supply you with amazing

alternatives to include flair to tasks small and large alike. Cricut machines give sharp masks for detailed etching on antiques and metal jewelry, as well as large stencils around 12" by 24" for decorating large surfaces like walls and furniture.

Thorough leatherwork.

Leather is in vogue, and cricut makes precision leather crafts a great deal more accessible than ever. Use the cricut knife blade™ to reduce on an range of grades, including full grain, split, and extra thick. To find the perfect leather for your job, browse the cricut leather collection.

Cards that link.

There is like a customized card to show care. Bring many distinct materials together like cardstock, crepe paper, cosmetic papers, corrugated cardboard, foil, or fabric to produce a unique composition. Cards are easy to design, fast to create, and perfect for virtually any function.

Perfect printables.

Create custom-printed stickers, stickers, and iron-ons in moments. Just use your printer to print designs on your own fabric of choice, then utilize the printing subsequently cut feature in design space® to reduce them about. Print decal paper, vinyl, iron-on, in addition to magnetic sheet.

Fabulous furniture.

Let us face it, it is tricky to find furniture that conveys your awareness of style. Together with cricut, you can certainly do something about it. Add a plastic theme in your dresser, add texture and colour into a table, or dress up your favorite chair. It doesn't take much to turn your furniture into something fantastic.

CHAPTER FIVE

EASY CRICUT PROJECT
IDEAS

Easy Method When Building any DIY Giant Paper Flower

Supplies you may need/want for large newspaper flowers

- Glue-gun

- 65-pound Card-stock

- 18 gauge wire

- Wire clippers

- Scissors or cutting machine (Cricut Explore Air two Machine)

- Lean wooden dowel for rolling

- 3-inch ring punch

- Fringe scissors(discretionary)

- Paper blossom template

Patience

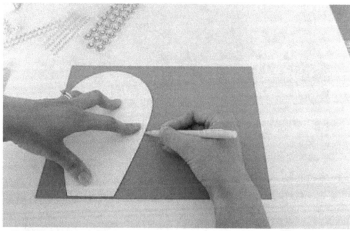

I'm using my Everly design template inside this tutorial, I am providing free of charge for your requirements once you subscribe! If you would like different things do not stressI've over 50 different giant blossom templates! Documents are all appropriate for cutting edge machines and simple to use for people that would like at hand-cut alternatively, that's the way I'll soon be using here. .

For hand-cut strategy - you'll need to print the templates in the own computer on huge cardstock slice on the templates and apply these to follow within the card that you use to really build the blossoms out of.

Step 1

- how to earn enormous paper flowers

Begin by placing you template onto your own card-stock of option and follow your own mane.

Large petal 1st coating -- 6 8 cuts

Medium petal second coating -- 6 7 cuts

Small petal 3rd coating -- 6 cuts

Extra little caked 4th coating -- 5 6 cuts

Note: in case you're employing our excess large everly design you'd begin with this xl petal as the 1 st coating and cut 7-8 petals.

Notes for users:

If you're using a cutting device that the cutting edge tool will expand the petals in their authentic format I save . To help with this I generated a petal design guide , which arouses paper usage. Plus below would be the petal dimensions in the event that you would rather plugin exact amounts.

Petal dimensions: extra-large 7.5 x 10.5 enormous 5.5 x 7.7 moderate 3.9 x 5.3 little 3.0 x 4.1 extra-small 2.5 x 3.7

If you're employing a machine jump right down to step 3.

Step 2

Once done these templates create In regards to a 13 inch blossom in diameter (Update: I have upgraded the freebie link above to generate a XL 17 inch blossom! Yay!) . You always have the option to ship the PDFs on a printer and also have them expanded for larger blossoms or put in an excess coating of XL petals.

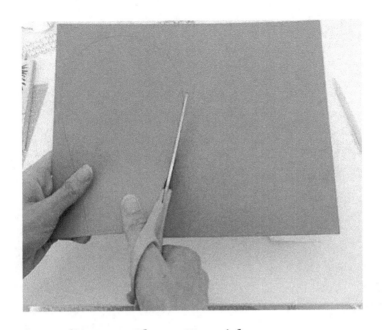

Spring Tulip Paper Flower Tutorial

DIY Paper Flower Pomander Balls

Step-by-step Paper Peony Tutorial

Cut all of your petals out when You Have completed .

You can create this process faster by piling up 2 3 Sheets ontop of oneanother and cutting on out several at the same time. Use binder clips to keep document out of going

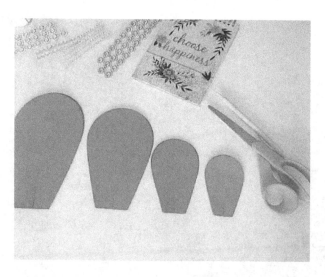

Step 3

Step 3

Now you need to cut slits at the base

Centre of each and every, roughly an inch, marginally less on small hills.

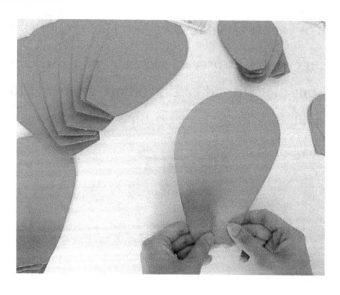

Step 4

Now beginning with the first coating put adhesive onto the interior border and over-lap the slit, however, perhaps not too much or your own hairline will likely be tight when constructed to receive all of the more compact layers inside. Try that with the petals. You are able to more than lap a bit more over the 3rd & 4th coating

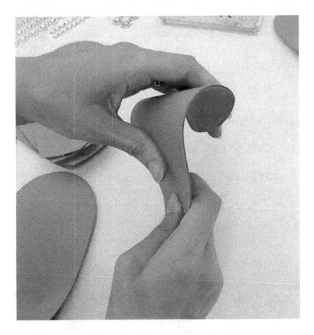

Step 5

Then next you'll flake out all of the swimsuit backagain. You are able to certainly do This manually or make use of a thick timber doul or perhaps a fat

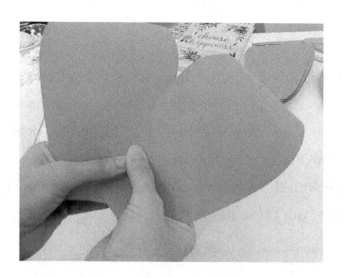

Pencil works also

Step 6

Assembly moment. You start with your 1st coating foundation Petals, you wish to bring a little glue into the outer border of a single petal and simmer to lap a second petal at roughly a 4-5' angel and then press firmly to get a second or 2.

Continue in this manner until all of the bottom petals meet together forming a ring at the middle of this blossom. See the angel of positioning as you move around ensuring you leave room enough for those petals in the future along equally at the close of the circle.

Step 7

Make use of a ring cut or punch a little square if you don't need you to Glue over the spacious floor.

Step 8

Begin the second layer of petals

Switching between your bottom petals as exhibited previously

Step 9

Carry on alternating petals including another coating

Step 10

Carry on alternating reds adding the 4th coating.

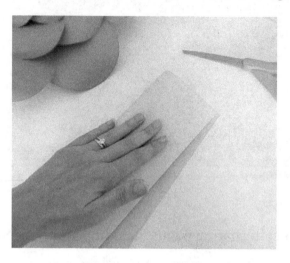

Step 11

To make the wrapped centre fold a piece of card stock in half span Wise, slice the paper down the center. Lay the two bits at the top another and fold in half .

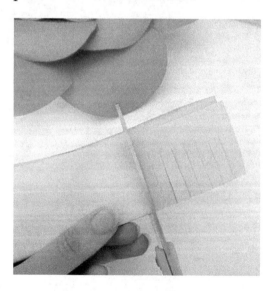

Step 12

Begin trimming slits all of the way down the paper. You can achieve this using regular scissors of course should you would like to earn the process easier it is possible to always catch this superb nifty strand scissors.

Separate both bits after you're through-cutting all of the slits.

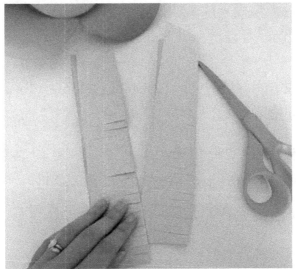

Separate the two pieces after you are through cutting all the slits.

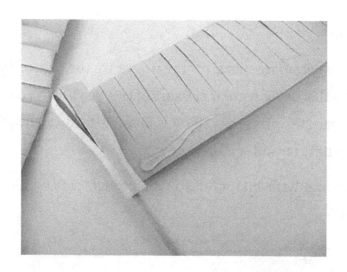

Step 13

Starting rolling the very first piece adding adhesive across the border as you can go.

Optional--you also may utilize the dowel to generate the rolling easier.

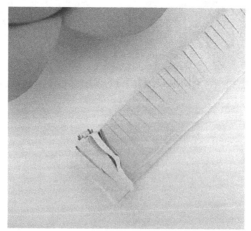

Once you complete rolling up the initial bit Keep on by incorporating on the Second one.

Glue the centre in and respect you pretty blossom! I expect you've liked this tutorial that will assist you to learn to earn large paper blossoms!

CHAPTER SIX
HOW TO EDIT CRICUT PROJECTS

C ricut layout space DOESN'T Autosave your jobs, therefore (as a superb practice), I suggest that you save your project after you put the specific initial slice, contour, or picture on the canvas region.

Occasionally, tasks may take some moment, and in case you not economize Your project as possible, your precious time and valuable work will cover a trip to the crap if Design Space Crashes.

I have missing a couple of moments prior to assessing my lesson, therefore, please conserve as you proceed. Notice:" I spare alterations in my project every five minutes or so.

When you begin on a Brand-new Canvas, then the save option (found on the top graded right-hand corner of this window) will most likely be greyed out, nevertheless whenever you place in an image, it is very likely to trigger.

To rescue your job, place the exact first thing (text, image, Contours, etc.) you may utilize in your canvas.

When you click save, a tiny window will pop up asking you to name your own work. If you're merely using Cricut pictures or fonts, then you will get the choice to go over your project Facebook or maybe Pinterest.

However, in the event you use your personal images, Subsequently the"Public" option won't appear. Do not worry though; you remain able to analyze your creations in the"My jobs" window that can I show you in the future.

After naming your job, click Save. A blue banner ads will look on this window, notifying you that the project is saved.

Now, you can begin changing your Style by incorporating Text, altering colours. In this scenario, I simply altered the colour of this document.

Nothing complicated.

Just don't forget to put away your function every three to five minutes; expect me, you do not wish to waste time at case the app crashes.

If at any stage you'd love to generate a fresh job, ensure that your project is stored.

No worries, yet.

If for any reason that you still have unsaved alterations, style space could produce a warning.

Do not simply take this warning lightly; at case that you click "replace" rather than"save" you'll lose your hard work.

It occurred to mepersonally, and it may happen to you!

Open function in cricut design space desktop

To begin a job, you have established, you would like a fresh and clean new canvas.

Presently, there is not a strategy for one to combine jobs. Let us expect cricut adds this operation shortly.

It is very likely to detect your allure in two distinct manners.

The first and quickest one is simply clicking the"my projects" shortcut located on the perfect corner corner of this window.

The next method is by simply clicking the projects choice on the remaining picture, and visit the drop-down menu then choose the alternative"my projects" (browse the many options of this drop-down menu to discover ready cut jobs)

As you are able to see on the screenshot above, the project I developed is correct there. The arrangement of these jobs it is based on the preceding date.

From the"my projects" view, you can edit, delete, customize, and reduce your formerly established tasks.

There are unique places you're able to click a specific job; should you click the"share" option, you'll be prompted to give a description, photographs, etc.. And if you click on the 3 dots (bottom-right of every activity), then you're likely to have the ability to delete it manually.

If you wish to customize your work or reduce it in once, then you are going to need to click on the included picture of your own design.

Upon clicking a very small window will begin, and you're going to be able to chat around and see all the information regarding the endeavor, such as the fonts, shapes, and pictures you've .

First and foremost, by that window, you have the capability to customize your project or send it to reduce the"make it" shortcut is fantastic as though your project was produced, it is possible to skip all of the design space procedure and realize the mat preview right away.

But, at the occasion that you wish to edit the overall look of your layout, click customize.

Now let us find out how to edit your undertaking!

Edit jobs in cricut design space desktop

After you click personalize for any job, you may be able to edit and change things around.

Require a peek in the subsequent screenshot to discover the adjustments I made into the first layout.

Add form: insert a circle in the picture and change colour.

Weld: pick the first picture and click the weld instrument (origin of the layers panel) to have each one our layout in 1 layer.

Twist: launch the plotted image in the center of the ring then select either, the ring then listen to click the slice tool (with the weld instrument).

Maintain the purple ring having an cut-out picture.

This editing is easy, I am confident you can perform, but what I needed to show is the perfect way to move after editing function.

Here is the item, in the event you click on rescue you'll reevaluate your principal design and when this is exactly what you need good. But in the event that you still need to maintain the task that you started with, click on save and pick the option"save"

After you click"save" you are likely to be more prompted to modify the title of your principal project; within this situation, I simply added a"2" into the name.

Easy, right?

However, if you opt to utilize either layout , return to your jobs and see some are readily available.

Save, open & edit projects from cricut design space app (ipad, phone).

The measures you want to shop, edited it, then begin work in cricut's program are astoundingly like people which you'd make from that pc.

You can find out it quite fast, but I wish to inform you I

scaled several white hair looking for every one of the choices, so here I'm to make it simple for you.

Let us find out together!

Save project at cricut design space program

The cricut design space app includes three specific viewpoints, home, canvas, and create.

Ordinarily, when you begin the program, the opinion will be put into"home." to begin focusing on a brand-new project, click on the blue square with all the and indication tap"canvas."

To be in a position to save your work, you have to set at least 1 thing (type, text, picture). For purposes of the tutorial, I used the picture #m44919.

After setting a product, tap on the save icon situated on the upper-left corner of the plan, and choose the option"save"

When you tap save just a tiny window will pop up where you will have the ability to put in the title of your job, and in which you would really like to save your endeavor.

Pick "save cloud" in case you would like to input your jobs in the pc, and you've gotten a trusted online connection. Choose"save iPad/iPhone" at the event you don't have trusted internet and enjoy having the capability to utilize offline.

When selecting"save iPad," you won't possess the capacity to discover folks tasks on your computer. But you're very likely to have the ability to use that task again and again with no web web.

I select"save cloud" since I love having availability to my jobs in my private pc. However, by all means, pick whatever matches your wants the best.

Save changes as you run in your style as in case the program crashes, you may drop all your hard labour.

1 thing to think about is that the best way to start a new project whenever you have something in your canvas. (it took me a while to figure it out)

See the "house" view and tap "new project." if you happen to have unsaved modifications, the program provides a warning. Select previews and rescue all the alterations and replicate the exact same approach to eliminate any hint.

Do not simply take this warning lightly; in the event you don't save, your project will most likely be missing.

Open Function in Cricut Design Space Program

To begin an already recognized Job, first, be sure that your Canvas is sterile (no more additional tasks, text, layout, or contours) and proceed into the"House" perspective of the strategy.

With this particular perspective, and bellow Your profile image, there is a Drop-down menu, then click then choose where your project is (Cloud or Ipad/iPhone).

Notice: by that drop-down (also if you're regarding the web) menu, then you might even find ready to reduce jobs, no cost tasks on your system, etc..

As the majority of my jobs are from the cloud, therefore I picked"my computer jobs round the cloud."

As you are able to see from the screenshot down below, I will come across the jobs I have been working through this tutorial.

Outstanding!

From that perspective,"home/my jobs from the cloud," you can conduct two or three things on each and every undertaking.

If you tap on the"chat" alternative, you'll be prompted to deliver a description, photographs, etc.. Your endeavor. And, in case that you click on the 3 dots (bottom-right of every activity), then you're likely to have the ability to delete it manually.

If you would really like to customize your work or reduce it in once, then you are going to need to tap the featured picture of your layout.

Upon tapping the perspective your telephone will change and you're going to be in a position to observe all the information regarding the endeavor, such as the fonts, shapes, and graphics you've .

First and foremost, from that window, you are able to personalize your project or send it to reduce the"make it" shortcut is good as though your project was produced, it is possible to skip all of the design space procedure and realize the mat preview immediately.

But, in case that you would really like to edit the overall look of your layout, click"customize".

Now let us find out how to edit your own project!

Edit Jobs in Cricut Design Space Program

If you tap customize for virtually any job, you'll have the ability to edit and change things around.

Require a peek in the subsequent screenshot to discover the adjustments I made into the first layout.

Select all the letters within this"daydream outline"

Weld each one of the internal letters.

Twist the outline of this coat along with the letters which are welded.

Notice: slice and weld are within the activity menu.

This editing is quite straightforward, I am certain that you can do much better, but exactly what I wished to show is the perfect way to move after viewing an already recognized job.

In the event you faucet rescue, you then are going to reevaluate your principal design and when this is exactly what you need good. But in the event that you still need to maintain the task that you started with, click on save and pick the option"save"

After you click"save" you are likely to be more prompted to alter the title of your principal job; within this situation, I simply added a"2" into the name.

Easy, right?

The alternatives are completely infinite about the specific cartridge. Users may even chase the 15 cartridges that maximize the potpourri basket cricut cartridge, even though they are considering certain particular themes and images. When it may have begun as a mere teaser cartridge, though the potpourri basket cricut cartridge shows that this is the type of innovative tool which may be the cricut client's paradise.

Cricut private cutters are taking hand crafts into a new degree. Individuals throughout the united states are amazed at the astonishing and innovative cricut ideas this system may result in a work listing. It is likely to create virtually anything awesome and one of a kind with all the cricut cartridges.

How does a cricut devices function? It is rather straightforward. Simply put in a cricut cartridge to the apparatus, then choose what colour card that you'd really prefer to use to your own private design and cut off. Each capsule consists of different themed layouts from seasonal layouts to favorite cartoon characters. You're in a position to pick out of the clip layouts to use for decorations, picture frames, picture frames, picture frames, picture frames, picture frames, picture frames, picture frames, picture frames, picture frames, picture frames, picture frames, picture frames, picture frames, picture frames, picture frames, picture frames, customized greeting cards, wall hangings, calendars and much more.

One of the superb cricut ideas it's extremely possible to make as your private craft is the cricut calendar. Each month can be created from another page and you are very likely to have the ability to decorate these pages using different layouts. Couldn't it be fantastic to make your February page working with the love struck season cartridge? The Easter cartridge will supply you unlimited designs to the April page calendar. The may calendar can be drawn up at the mother's day cartridge. How interesting is it to design your July webpage with trimmings made in the independence day season cartridge? December might be equipped with all the joys of the season cartridge along with snow friends cartridge. You might choose to a heart's content.

Another good idea you are ready to possibly make is your scrapbook. This well-loved craft task is the reason cricut cutting machine was invented in the very first site. Considering all of the cricut cutting edge gear, you have the ability to personalize scrapbooks for your kids, such as mother-daughter or daddy and kid keepsake. Cricut created capsules which each and every little child would delight in generating such as the once upon a princess cartridge or even the Disney tinker bell and friends cartridge. Your little hero will certainly adore the batman layout in the batman: the brave and the bold or robotz cartridges. Cricut provides you humungous designs to choose from the scrapbooking ideas.

The cricut layouts aren't only lay out ideas but additionally fonts and alphabets in the sesame street font cartridge and the Ashlyn's alphabet cartridge. Use these exciting tools when creating your personalized present like a wall-hanging image frame of experiencing a photo of a memorable event of the recipient of your gift. Embellish your walls dangling with quite cutouts made with this cricut cutter.

Your cricut notions are endless through the machine in addition to the cricut capsules to coincide with every occasion and occupation which it is likely to take into consideration. Creating a cricut project along with the comprehensive household is a great way to spend time together and producing these magnificent things are sometimes a fantastic experience for everyone to achieve.

Finest strategies for selecting the ideal cricut personal electronic cutter

The assortment of cricut personal digital cutter machines

has been made to automate a lot of these fiddly crafting tasks. In case you haven't heard of those sooner, then continue reading at the event you would love to understand how to maintain your home crafts to the following level. If you are aware of them, you may be asking yourself the way to choose which of those cutting edge machines is acceptable for you. Within another manual, I will be assisting you to pick which among those four cricut models is the ideal match for your requirements. In the process, you're extremely likely to understand the advantages and disadvantages of every machine, which often means you're in a position to create an educated decision.

The four versions we're likely to be thinking about will be the regular cricut personal electronic cutter, the cricut create, the cricut expression and the cricut cake.

The simplest variant to test in the beginning is that the cricut cake. This differs to other folks, since it's created with one goal in your mind. That is, to make professional looking decorations. It may cut shapes from bread, fondant, gum paste along with other raw materials. It is quite similar to this cricut expression system, but the functioning parts are altered to make them suitable for meals. That means components that need to be cleaned may be easily removed. If you're seeking to make edible decorations, then that's the sole alternative in the range. This version retails from roughly $270.

The extra three cricut personal electronic cutter models are suitable for printing. They cut out of the specific same materials, such as card, paper, vinyl and vellum. Which version you choose will depend on your budget and requirements.

Budget

The regular cricut personal digital cutter is your cheapest priced at the scope, costing at about $100.

Next upward is the cricut produce, starting from $160 and upward.

At the top of this scope variant is the cricut expression, which will set you back roughly $225.

Prerequisites

All models are harmonious with the entire choice of cricut cartridges. This typically means you have got an almost infinite supply of cutting edge designs, since you could always buy more capsules. So there are two big facets on your should push your selection. These may be the dimensions of cuts and machine, along with the variety of cutting edge choices.

The traditional personal electronics cutter and produce servers are small and mobile. They'll cut shapes about 11.5 inches. The produce has a substantially wider assortment of cutting edge capabilities.

The expression is a bigger machine, made to acquire a permanent place in a desk or workbench. It will cut shapes to about 23.5 inches, along with using a massive assortment of cutting edge works.

By taking into consideration these factors, you are going to need to be able to select which cricut personal electronic cutter is the one for you.

Folks actually believe the cricut method are the 1 instrument that is in charge of the conceptualization of these designs which we find in scrapbooks. In reality, the designs derive in the mind of the user and so are created concrete by the cricut cutting system.

Additionally, it also there are distinct tools which produce the designs like capsules and applications programs. The ideal software program out there's that the cricut design studio. With this system, you are able to edit and create your individual designs and edit present designs that are pre - packed.

Life is great indeed! People also feel that the usage of a cricut cutting procedure is simply restricted to the subject of scrapbooking. Just a few women and guys know about the nevertheless there that the cricut machine in addition to the cartridges along with the software tools might be used to find a significant selection of items. You will encounter a whole lot of cricut projects it's very likely to utilize the cricut cutting platform for and just your mind can limit what you could do.

Greeting cards are excellent cricut jobs for anybody to

share in. Considering all the designs you are going to be able to acquire from the cricut cartridge together with the software programs that you have set up, you design covers which withstand the unconventional. The problem that many people experience when they attempt to buy greeting cards is that nearly all of the time is that they can't track down the design of their card they are looking for. This might cause anxiety and a wonderful deal of frustration about the customer's part. You are a great deal better off making your personal greeting cards.

Cricut calendars are only another fantastic thought to get a cricut cutting apparatus. A calendar is full of 12 weeks. You might get creative and search for layouts on your own cartridge or applications that will reflect the entire month that is on your calendar. If we're in the month of December, then you might find designs which match the mood and feel of December. Start looking for snowmen, reindeers, and christmas trees. I guarantee you that you have each the designs you'll ever desire inside your cartridge or applications.

Bear in mind, only your creativity can restrict what you do. These cricut jobs may possibly be used either for individual satisfaction or revenue generating functions. Be imaginative with your favorite machine. You never know what crazy and angry ideas can pop into your own mind.

This report explains the several uses of the cricut jukebox system, however, a justification on the cricut system, known as the personal electronics monitoring system will probably be in order. The cricut personal cutter is a whole cutting system utilized for crafting. It's lightweight and made to aid with your house, office or college scrapbooking and other tasks. It is fairly user friendly and incredibly convenient. As a plug in, cut and layout machine, it's totally beneficial to people focusing on card creating scrapbook building and possibly even paper crafting.

But, the cricut cutter system requires capsules to get the task finished. It many individual capsules to lessen designs of any sort and some other measurement, depending on the collection of the user. Cartridges are a great deal of that everybody is able to shell out a great deal of time loading and reloading individual capsules to operate with. To be in a place to be unique designs and cut them back you want to change from 1 pill to a different, which may be rather time consuming. However, there's 1 machine made to decrease the problem of loading and reloading, or changing of capsules - voila! - the revolutionary cricut jukebox machine.

What is this cricut jukebox apparatus? It's a very valuable equipment, valuable to anybody engaged in the craft of producing and crafting. Cricut jukebox, that resembles a easy cartridge, is not just a box. It's a system or instrument which, when plugged in the cricut cutter system, may provide six (6) capsules of layouts that are unique and dimensions. Apparently, the vast array of these 6 capsules must be up for your liking and needs. This program will certainly offer you a hand on your designing and cutting jobs. The jukebox facilitates and gets rid of the problem of changing in and from capsules onto your own cricut machine.

There are more features of the machine you want to learn about. This cricut jukebox system might also be searchable. Which meansyou can function with more than 1 jukebox whilst working in your cricut machine. Taking into consideration the jukebox system provides a exceptional characteristic that empowers three jukeboxes to be used in the particular very same instant, you have gotten the way of using more capsules whenever you have the need to. 1 jukebox holds 6 capsules, so consequently, if you simultaneously use 3 jukeboxes at 1 time, you'll have 18 capsules ready to utilize. How do that? Every cricut jukebox is outfitted with cable wires - a very straightforward process to follow. Just plug 1 jukebox in your own cricut apparatus and plug into another jukebox on the very first one that you attachedinto the key cricut device, which you move, a jukebox plugged, one after another. To put it differently join one using another - simple!

Another great characteristic of the jukebox, is that it is possible to stack them to minimize place on your office, letting you operate safely in minimal distance - and much longer, it supplies a compartment where you may safely pile your capsules. The cricut jukebox procedure is portable and easy to execute, so, you have got advantage in addition to simplicity of usage. It is not significant to hang to individual altering of capsules, the moment you are in a position to make the most of simply pushing buttons, and keeping cartridges of your choice from the tip of your fingers!

Although, apparently each of the variations of cricut cutting machines operate in a similar method to some extent using just a great deal of variation into the particular exact same design and characteristics, the cricut layout has emerged as a flexible platform that has altered the crafting sector by introducing a few new features that enhance its performance.

The cricut machine allows users to reduce many letters, words and shapes to blue dimensions for classroom décor, signage, scrapbooks, and a great deal more.

CHAPTER SEVEN
TRICKS FOR USING THE
CRICUT MACHINE

L et us guarantee that you are not missing any merchandise.

If anything isn't included either reunite your explore air two to the store where you purchased it get cricut support to get a fast replacement.

If you've got anything extra, well, that's simply an excellent bonus!

Your package should at least include these:

Education manual.

Cricut cutting mat.

Cutting sword (pre-installed)

Cricut explore air 2 (if you're missing this, the box was probably quite mild)

Electricity + USB strings

Silver pen + accessory adapter (pre-installed)

Cardstock + vinyl samples (we've heard of a couple kits overlooking these)

Notice: there are several different kits available (premium vinyl, ultimate kit, tools kit, complete starter kit, vinyl starter kit) so you might have a few additional things contained.

Contrasts between the explore air and explore air 2

A frequent question I'm asked is: the explore air and explore air 2 look fundamentally the specific same and seem to receive all the exact same features so... What's the difference? The remedy is: rate and colour. The explore air two carries a 2x quick manner which operates with vinyl, iron-on, and cardstock. Additionally, it comes in 3 very colors: mint green, white, pastel pink, and sky blue. That's it!

Now let's have a glimpse inside.

Inside the cricut explore air 2

Here I shall cover the basic features of the explore air two, and a few of them are nifty. The outline below is of the very first explore air but that the layout is entirely the same. Just envision the fairly mint finish.

Tool cup -- retains pens, scissors, etc.. .

Accessory publish a. This is the stage in which the attachment adapter is pre-installed and where you can put in a pen for drawing instead of cutting-edge. Furthermore, it's useful for holding blades.

Blade clamp b. The blade comes pre-installed. In case you ever need to replace it or eliminate parts of vinyl, then that is the location where you'd love to look.

Accessory storage compartments. Apart from the instrument cup, the explore air 2 comprises two storage compartments. The wheels on the left keeps additional blade housings, blades, together with the attachment adapter. It sports a magnetic strip to keep replacement blades protected and free of rolling about. The larger compartment is fantastic for conserving more tools/pens.

Smart position dial. Rotate the dial to select the substance you are likely to be cutting off. It appears fantastic to reverse and indicates which substances you have the ability to cut with 2x fast method.

Cutting mat. This will be how we load most things to our cricut machine. It's sticky on one side for holding our material securely in place.

A brief notice regarding the blade and attachment clamps: if you have to carry out the attachment or blade clamp just pull open the lever and pull on the metallic casing. The blade sits on the inside and there's a tiny plunger on the surface. You may press on this to demonstrate the blade that is magnetically saved out. In case you have to replace the blade just pull it out and drop another one in.

To use a pencil only open attachment clamp a, dip it down in, then shut the clamp.

Ok, let's get your machine connected and put up the

necessary drivers.

Joining your own platform for your pc/mac/iPad

Even though the cricut explore air 2 might be utilized we are going to start with setting up this with the USB cable. Start by placing it on a face with 10″ available behind it because the cutting edge pad will move back and forth within the machine.

Twist the apparatus in, connecting the electricity adapter and the USB cable.

Switch on your explore air two system along with your pc.

Proceed to the cricut website and register an individual account and find the most recent plugin program.

Run the installer and see design.cricut.com.

Click on the menu icon in the top left corner and choose new machine setup. You will be guided through the installation process and your very first task, a thank you card.

Light traction (blue)

Construction paper

Mild cardstock

Printer + scrapbook paper

Vellum

Standard grip (green)

Regular + embossed cardstock

Heat transfer (iron-on) + standard vinyl

Window clings

Vinyl

Strong grip (purple)

Endorsed cloth

Chipboard

Corrugated cardboard

Leather suede

Foam

Magnetic fabric

Posterboard

Wood (such as balsa)

This is a bundle of helpful tools that you can buy straight from cricut. It includes:

Scissors. (self-evident)

Tweezers. All these are reverse-grip so that you squeeze the handle to open and release to close. Super useful for holding tasks together since they dry alongside a thousand other mini functions.

Scraper. Crucial for working collectively with vinyl and cleanup the cutting mat.

Spatula. Used to lift material out of the cutting mat.

Weeder. Helps remove vinyl from its lining or removing tiny small cuts.

If you don't have those tools, I strongly recommend either purchasing the bundle from cricut or buying cricut explore air 2 bundle which contains them. They need to run you around $15 if purchased as a set.

Implementing the cricut explore air 2: your first layout

In your computer, if you've followed the"new machine setup, then" from before you should pay a visit to a design set on the screen. If you don't locate the plan excursion design.cricut.com. Click on the menu icon in the top left corner and choose new machine setup.

You will wish to have handy: the included sample cardstock, newspaper, cutting mat, together with your silver pen. In the event that you still have the protective film on your cutting mat remove it now and put it aside for later. It has to be maintained for protecting the surface since you are not using it.

Load that the gray cardstock on to the very mat. Along with the textured side facing upwards, line it up vertically on the mat. It has to be lined on the top left corner, just under the cricut logo.

Load the mat into the machine. Insert the mat accord with all the mat guides, here's a picture to learn precisely what it should look like. Keep the mat pressing firmly against the pliers while still pressing the"load/unload" button on the very top of the machine. The icon looks like a set of double-arrows.

Add the silver pen. Open accessory clamp a. Afford the pencil cap and place it tip-down into your house until the arrow on the pen disappears. Go ahead and close the clamp. Tip: place the cap in the end of the pen when trimming so you don't lose it.

Evaluate the design on the mat preview screen. Press go.

· establish the dial on your device to cardstock.

· the"c" button onto the system has to be uninstalled. Press it to commence the program and see the magic happen!

· unload the mat. After the task is finished press the load/unload button and then remove the pencil. I usually keep mine in the compartment, but there's also the convenient bin round the left of the machine if you'd rather have simple accessibility.

· place the cutting mat face down on a clean surface and then curl up the border it. The fabric should peel off from the mat, and as you pull it off just keep bending the mat up to create this somewhat easier.

Twist the card creasing it. Do the same with your blue newspaper and place within the grey card. You may glue this setup in the event that you would like.

Tada, your final product should look like this:

Cricut access

Cricut availability is an excellent subscription service supplied by cricut. Dependent on the application you choose you're given unlimited (but temporary) access to fonts, designs, or maybe a 10% discount on all purchases from cricut.com

Cricut access may unquestionably be rewarding if you wind up purchasing a fantastic deal of things from the cricut design space store.

Personally, I love to purchase designs like I need them and this way i've got them eternally.

Bluetooth utilize

The research air 2 features bluetooth in the box so it will use your computer wirelessly, either your iphone, or your ipad. In case you need aid pairing it with your computer, cricut has an excellent page which covers windows/mac/ios/android devices.

Tricks and tips

It's possible to utilize design space with essentially any image you find. Check out cricut's step-by-step instructions.

If you'd like pictures to use i've constructed an excellent group of free svg pictures that you might import.

Always make a test cut, on a very small quantity of material. It takes an extra moment but it might save as much money in the event you've obtained your tastes calibrated erroneously or if your blade is gunky.

You can use the explore air 2 without a internet link should you place it using an ios (iphone/ipad) or android device.

14 bonus cricut tutorials

I have put together my 14 favorite cricut tutorials for beginners, experts, and everyone in between.

Each tutorial is super easy, enjoyable, and explains each the little details that could surely make or break your design.

Most are videos nevertheless there are a few of text tutorials sprinkled in.

Some of those projects you are likely to be generating: disney tee, DIY stickers, personalized mugs, and 3d pop up art!

Implementing the cricut explore air (beginner-level)

DIY custom stickers using the cricut explore air

If you haven't seen this yet you're in for a treat. Auntie tay goes on the best way best to make personalized stickers. All these are amazing for spouses, business promos, or maybe you're like me rather than really grew up!

The Way To Wash Your Own Cricut Cutting Mat (And Restick It Afterwards) How To Clean Your Mat (Process 1: Gentle Cycle)

When you discover your cricut mat isn't any more sticky enough to properly suspend your material, try these out approaches to clean your mat and breathe a while back into it.

Since your mat accumulates dirt and debris with your loving usage, proceed down the list to more potent cleaning processes.

Be gentle with your own mats, plus they may even last you through numerous rounds of holiday parties.

Sticky lint roller

Run a sticky lint roller (or fold of masking tape) through your cricut mat to get rid of dust, fibers, bits of paper, in addition to hairs.

This is sometimes performed every day, involving tasks, when you fail to cover your cricut mats or simply whenever you discover fibers and pieces collecting on your own mat.

It's an excellent way to remove any residual slivers or even pieces of paper, instead of trying to truly go after them with tweezers. Following the lint roller or masking tape is more powerful regarding the mat, then it pulls all the offending hairs and parts of paper straight off the mat! It works especially well on the less-tacky cutting mats.

Safe to your pink cricut fabric grip mats!

Baby wipes

· gently wash down with unscented, alcohol-free, bleach-free baby wipes. Lotion-free, cornstarch-free. You desire the full plainest wipes you will find, so you're not coat your cutting mats with additional creams, oils or solvents that may hinder the stickiness or divide the paste.

· let dry ahead of using.

Soap and hot water

Wash with soap and warm water.

Dish soap is your best to use, and you desire to use soap that is free of lotions that may gunk your mat.

Gently scrub using a cloth, soft brush, soft sponge, or magic eraser, and wash well.

Permit dry completely before using.

Caution : do not use very hot water, as heat was demonstrated to warp cricut mats, making it so they won't fit nicely in your own system.

The outcomes

Frequently enough, simply washing your mat will likely be sufficient to rejuvenate its first tacky glory! After your cutting mat includes completely dried, have a look at its stickiness working with a scrap of the substance you are likely to use for your next task, or even a clean finger.

If your mat has weathered enough seasons of jobs, or been washed and scrubbed one a good deal of occasions, you need to become something somewhat stronger...

The way to clean your mat (strategy 2: heavy duty)

If these gentle cleaning methods don't revive your cutting mat performance, you can try breaking out the big guns and use adhesive remover to completely wash your mat.

The cleaning processes found on this page are not to the pink cricut fabric grip mat. They are for the blue, green, and purple cricut mats. Don't put anything moist (such as water) on your pink fabric mats.

What is adhesive remover?

Glue removers are strong solvents that could dissolve a few of the glue (the sticky paste) on your mat, helping you eliminate each the gunk that is stuck right into it.

Caution : this process will strip your cutting mat of adhesive, so you may want to reapply adhesive to restick your own mat. Do not worry, i'll assist you .

Which glue remover should you utilize?

I advocate with goo gone because it's been repeatedly and employed by the cricut and crafting community. However, you don't have to acquire a very different product for this! In the event you have any kind of adhesive remover lying around that you're knowledgeable about, it will most likely work just fine.

Added alternatives are:

70% isopropyl (rubbing) alcohol

De-solv-it universal stain remover & pre-wash

La's totally awesome all objective concentrated cleaner

The finest approach to utilize adhesive remover to clean your cricut mat

Read the directions of your glue remover, and accommodate as required.

Pour or spray a small amount onto your mat.

Spread it around using a scraper, or a few other rigid piece of plastic like a timeless credit card.

Allow the lube sit and operate its own magic. The longer you allow the adhesive peel sit, the more material it will remove. The precise duration will depend on which solvent you use, so read the directions on your own bottle. If this is the first time, then I urge just it sit for a few moments to get rid of the filthy surface layer of glue. (if you've restuck you mat a great deal of occasions and are prepared for a fresh start, it is possible to let it sit for as much as 20-30 minutes)

Use your scraper into scrape on the filthy glue off your own mat. Perhaps you will wash it off with a paper or cloth towels.

6. · wash with soap and warm water to get rid of any lingering residue.

7. · allow the mat dry thoroughly

However, what does it mean to scrapbookers?

The use of cutouts and shapes in a variety of colours are a great way to enhance and add pizzazz to a variety of crafts and arts projects, such as scrapbooking and card making.

All these additionally known as diets might be of a myriad of substances, including card stock, vellum, lean plastics, foils and transparencies.

With nearly all of manual and digital cutters available on the market nowadays, like the sizzix and cricut expression, you need to plan ahead of time and select the color of your die-cut prior to cutting. To put it differently, the color of your style will be the color of this paper (or fabric, or inventory) you pick.

In as a result, when creating complex or elaborate layouts, you may need to change paper colours frequently.

Added systems, such as the wish blade, let you print your preferred shape with a standard inkjet printerthan run onto the printed page through the system to reduce. The largest issue for this is that it's a two step process, using two distinct machines, which requires the consumer properly setup registration marks so that the machine will know just where to cutback. This is often a trial and error procedure and the results are not always satisfactory.

Thus, the requirement is present for a system that permits the consumer to publish a picture and lessen the image without manual registration. This is the point where the cricut picture comes in, to meet with a huge gap in the current market and open an entirely new world of possibilities for scrapbookers, cardmakers and paper crafters generally.

Main cricut picture characteristics:

With cricut pattern and cricut color cartridges, you are able to fill any shape with exquisite patterns, including

More dimension and number into your designs;

You can use all previous cartridges with the cricut picture. But there'll also be new cartridges released to function just with this new device, just like it happened with the cricut cake;

The cricut picture can also be compatible with both the gypsy and the design studio software;

Each the information can be easily accessed by employing aLCD touch-screen navigation program;

New capsules for your cricut picture include: 12 new cricut picture art cartridges and 12 new cricut picture colors & patterns cartridges;

The on-board colour and pattern selector lets you choose colors, sizes and even more;

The cricut picture machine may cut contours from.25" to 11.5", also functions with large-format papers around 12" x 12";

Just like the cricut expression along with other preceding machines, the picture does not expect a computer to function;

Share the very same blades and blade housings as another cricut machines, making it simple for users to update without having to purchase everything;

The only different is that the mat, which is greatly improved.

This means no longer no more purchasing a lot of expensive scrapbook paper, shifting paper colours between fighting or cuts guide registration marks. Whatever you'll need in one simple to use system which does all for you and empowers your creative to soar.

The cricut picture isn't just unique to the crafting business, but to the area of technology. Currently there is no another system that incorporates both printing and cutting how the picture does.

The best exotic cutters are cricut machines

A cricut machine does not want a computer port. The cricut die cutters are free standing machines that produce precision cut designs in card stock paper. All these cricut die cutters are extremely popular with newspaper crafters and garbage book artists. A lot of designs are chosen by capsules to permit scrapbookers and musicians to create designs inside a chosen theme.

There are 3 different cricut machines available on the market. The most popular is that the cricut expression. Other variations include the cricut and the cricut create. These machines offer you several cartridge layouts such as cutouts for all 50 nations out of the US and perish discounts for wedding themed things.

The cricut personal digital cutter typically comprises the George cartridge. This cartridge delivers an entire group of fonts and basic shapes to get you started. Shapes include blackout, shadow, form, allure, slotted, in addition to signal. These contours can be highlighted in 12 specific sizes. The whole cricut private cutter package generally cost roughly $300.

The cricut expression sells for approximately $500.00 and uses the very same cartridges as the cricut private digital cutter. This system has the capability to cut to a 12"x24" mat. The larger cutting edge makes it ideal for big building projects.

The cricut create prices around $400.00 and will be precisely the exact same dimensions as the first cricut. However, with the cricut create, cut shapes and letters have a large format dimensions such as the cricut expression. The"Don Juan" starter capsule typically comprises this bundle. This cartridge offers multiple skins, shapes, and advanced capacities. This cartridge includes shadow, stitched, marquee, puzzled, and under stress contours.

Scrapbook artists love the cricut machines since it's such a superb investment. With a single cartridge, it's possible to literally replace the need to purchase sheet after sheet of alphabet stickers and shaped work outs. Having one cartridge you can design many distinct looks in numerous sizes. By adjusting to many different dimensions and paper options, the cricut machine can produce many distinct looks with a single cartridge.

One of the best characteristics of a cricut machine is its simplicity of use. School aged children can utilize the cricut method for design reports or projects for faculty. Cartridges typically offer approximately 250 deigns in 12 sizes. Furthermore, cricut supplies a whole lot of different cartridges. There's very little that you can't do with a cricut machine. They are fantastic for scrapbooking, artistry, faculty jobs, and sign making. The choices are endless with all the cricut machine.

4 things you need to know before purchasing!

The cricut and cricut expression house cutting machine have become an exciting key to any crafter and scrap booker's provide cabinet. Together with the machine's capacity to cut letters, shapes, and figures at the touch of a button, the cricut is a really easy ways to create scrapbooking pages, display boards, in addition to trendy wall art! The cricut manufacturer has made the system much more intriguing and innovative with the cricut design studio software. This system takes the cricut method to soaring levels of imagination. The program lets you hook up your cricut for your home computer and make countless new layouts and shapes for the apparatus to decrease.

The software comprises a searchable database of each letter, shape and amount in the entire cricut cartridge library, placing tens of thousands of designs at your fingertips. And, cricut delivers online updates to always raise the library collection. In addition, along with the tools included, you can acquire full control over your cricut, letting you meld (referred welding) letters into one word, and to format and structure objects on a virtual cutting mat prior to your machine starts its work.

A couple things to keep in mind about the cricut design studio software:

1. Though the program lets you see and design with any cartridge available on the marketplace, it is possible to just use the machine together with the cartridges you really have. The wonderful thing is that designing distinct things on the computer will supply you a clearer idea about exactly what cartridges you'd love to purchase next. Plus, you might save your designs for later use.

2. Possessing a daily creativity-wise? Want some fresh inspiration? Have a look at the cricut message boards or look for the net to check at and get the fashionable and imaginative

files that further cricut design studio users have established. This is a fantastic way to add unique layouts to your designs, but to also become fresh and new inspiration.

3. It's possible for you to generate a design with over 1 cartridge; you will merely need to have all of the capsules accessible once you're ready to cut off.

4. You're able to still create unique layers into your layouts, such as shadows and other components. The most vital issue is to make each component on a different layer in the design studio applications in order that your cricut system will likely understand to reduce these layers separately and on the newspaper of your choice.

The cricut design studio software retails for about 6 dollars, and it is a definite must have for any cricut enthusiast. The computer applications will loose all your creative thoughts and expand the cricut's skills to complete new levels.

In this world where the industry generally does not go your way, you'll have to optimize whatever manner you've got. I guarantee anybody that if you are put into a scenario that's life and death, all of your senses will tingle like"spiderman's spider - sense".

You will take a look at things from a more critical angle and your mind will function. From the area of scrapbooking, the cricut was connected with nothing more than simply making scrapbooks and nothing more. Butif you enlarge your vision and look at this wonderful tool from a company standpoint, you will notice the possibility this tool may have. As a matter of a fact, there is a great deal of revenue generating part-time tasks that you'll be able to take part in.

The cricut equipment includes with it a load of infinite possibilities including cricut jobs. People today look in the above-mentioned method as a mere tool for scrapbooking however if you look at it deeper, then you may observe it's capable of a whole lot longer. 1 use of the cricut equipment that could allow you to make profit is really invitations.

The front cover design of those greeting cards is really where a cricut machine will render its providers. With using a software program, you may start looking for designs which could fit the event the invitation is created for. If your invitation is for a baby shower, then you may start looking for a design that shows the picture of a baby shower and so many more.

Another the use of the cricut equipment is on producing cricut calendars. Each calendar has 12 months on it and you can use the cricut machine to reduce layouts that help exemplify the disposition related to a specific month. When it's halloween, you can search for design with jack - o - lanterns and spooky ghosts and a lot more. Greeting cards are where cricut machines may also be used for.

CONCLUSION

So you've mastered the cricut design studio, you are a professional crafter, your trash reservation skills are legendary, now what? Why not put you abilities to work for you. Here are five cricut suggestions that will put money in your pocket.

There are tens of thousands of happy crafters who love using their cricut die cutting platform, but haven't quite got the applications to work like they need, that's where you come in. You're able to take custom orders and produce cut files your clients can utilize inside their die cutter. Or, hang in craft forums and find out exactly what people want and then make those cut files and supply them on ebay.

Each home based business owner must market their site. Join networking groups or post your ceremony in forums or classified advertisements sites. So what is this money making idea? Begin a cricut vinyl ribbon service. We've got all seen mywebsite.com from the rear window of somebody's automobile, now you can produce plastic tips and assist individuals get clients to their site.

People are always searching for ways to include personalized accents to decor. So this is actually the subsequent money making idea. Proceed to the paint and wallpaper shops in your area and ask to leave your business cards set up a flyer advertising your custom made wall artwork support.

Telephone interior decorators and notify them you are able to customize any house decorating tasks together with your personalized wallies. These wall stickers can be any word, design, animation character, inspirational quote, symbols or numbers you produce with design studio and vinyl sheets or sheets.

Last but maybe not least because you are the local expert in regards to the cricut design studio use this understanding to educate others. Go to craft shops and also offer to teach a class from basic methods to advanced suggestions.

You love crafting it's an excellent hobby, but it might be pricey buying those supplies. With those 5 cricut thoughts you finally have a means to use your skills and expertise to help set the cost. Along with helping fellow arts and craft fans to express themselves using a bit of assistance from you. I expect you try all these very low cost start up tips to earn additional money using cricut software.

CPSIA information can be obtained
at www.ICGtesting.com
Printed in the USA
BVHW042226141020
591100BV00002B/5